# INTERESTING CASE STUDIES AND OTHER SELECT INFORMATION

First published Jul 23, 2017.

"It is neat to look at interesting cases." —Attributed to Aristotle

# INTERESTING CASE STUDIES

*by Nathan Coppedge*

A TRANSLATION OF HIPPOCRATES

*"Life is short, and Art long; the crisis fleeting; experience perilous, and decision difficult. The physician must not only be prepared to do what is right himself, but also to make the patient, the attendants, and externals cooperate."*

—Hippocrates

Section 1.

Study Chinese medicine (carefully), don't grow old.

Patients can be controlled (and helped!) by food, psychologically.

Section 2.

With sleep and onset, expectations are neither more nor less than is normal.

Avoid toxicities.

Good food is simple.

Serious patients recover.

There are signs with recovery.

Recovery requires belief.

The onset of illness must be carefully watched.

Patience is frequently the best cure.

Section 3.

Humans are not always apt to adapt, and they are more adapted to cold than heat.

People suffer the maladies of their age in life.

Section 4.

Become accustomed to the ugliness of medicine.

Disease has perplexing cases which are more subtle and generally less extreme.

In extreme cases watch out!

Section 5.

Have a healthy fear of death!

Sexy people reproduce.

Section 6.

Watch out for peculiarities; the cause may be something deadly.

Death is common or inevitable; immortality is rare or inexorable.

There are things worse than death.

Section 7.

Discoloration is unhealthy.

Good from bad is good, but bad from good is bad.

Good never comes from bad, although bad can come from good.

See also:

Magical requirement for panacea:

- To repair one's teeth, then to cure illness.

…

PANACEAS CHRONOLOGICAL ORDER:

Another panacea: 1881: Dimensions: Good architecture is a miracle pill.

Another panacea: 1901: I'm not in such good health myself might actually help cure problems. I'm not sure why.

Another panacea: 1919: You might be feeling blue in the face. Even I caught the virus. Except you're feeling fine, aren't you? Then did you? Accompanying painting of Falstaff: <u>Joie de vivre - Wikipedia</u>

Another panacea: 1921: Say: "Kind of scary ______
condition. I might be unlucky. Expect the expected. Soon
I will be kaput, lifeless, like a deformed corpse, I am
gasping for life."

Medical Integrations:

- Biological clock means immortality
  [Hippocrates?] Immortality where it
  occurs is 'inexorable'.

OTHER FIGURES OF ANCIENT MEDICINE:

- Basic Epicureanism: Known for saying
  'eat fish and avoid the worst suffering.'
- Advanced Epicureanism: "Refrain from
  drinking all citrus as it corrodes the
  organs and destroys the digestive
  acids". Katy Ruben notes it is good for
  killing a few parasites, then should be
  avoided. Majority vegetarians no
  longer need citrus. Nathan Coppedge
  notes that drinking lemonade may
  have been a contributing factor before
  developing schizophrenia in college.

...

NOTES:

Bile is often associated with corruption.

Bile and puss emerge from interactions between the body and invasive organisms, but can also occur naturally.

Corruption is a psychological interpretation of bile, or bad feeling.

Today bile is recognized to be an essential part of how the body works, but pus is usually considered a secondary characteristic of being unhealthy, as it generally only forms in wounds to aid healing.

...

## PARANOID EXPERIENCES

I've thought about this, and the voices in my head don't believe I live in the actual universe. It's upsetting.

We've all found the 'Cotswld Flour Baking Club'...

This is similar to the pop-up that appears if you visit a typical page explaining the properties of barley flour:

It's free to join The Cotsw ld Flour Baking Club!

Sign up today and get insider access to exclusive offers, rewards, event invites and new product alerts - and an introductory 10% off your next purchase online!

JOIN THE CLUB

This is from looking up if malt flour contains alcohol. (It doesn't).

Malt extract does sometimes.

I get it, they open that, and it spreads like a virus.

Oh no! I did that again!

It's just a virus.

You're paranoid schizophrenic, you're not paranoid.

That's the problem, you want to reproduce with a man. That's the only problem for you.

I get it: I need a psychologist, they need a doctor.

…

This might not be paranoia:

93 Orange Street New Haven, Connecticut, 5th Floor: I covered the air conditioner. But they still had drugs coming in through the window or something. Gave me waking nightmares after I had a weird dream about a painter who didn't know how to talk sensibly. I was worried I had overdosed without willfully taking drugs.

…

Possibly paranoid unless you are allergic:

Nathan made me integrate honey nut cheerios and they contain nuts!

- <u>What is the most comprehensive market study that has been done on millennial's?</u> (...)

I believe they test as liking science, wanting to make independent decisions. They have somewhat moderate tastes but splurge on things they prefer (for example, 3-d printing, or specialty beverages). They tend to be atheistic and roughly very pessimistic. They don't want to be fooled, but they are people of their times, and much of their life might have to do directly or indirectly with 'bill gates' / crypto currencies, 3-d printing, and scary occult magic.

- <u>What is an introductory case study with a theory application?</u> (...)

Sounds like someone is requesting you find one. Maybe they have one in mind.

If not, examples are sort of like:

- Zimbardo, the Stanford Prison Experiment.
- Stanley Milgram, Yale psychological experiments (remember, the tests were designed to test whether participants would keep shocking a 'victim' although the 'victim' was actually in on the experiment).
- The Third Wave experiment. A particular high school teacher tested whether students would begin behaving like Nazis under certain conditions. The results were not good.

- <u>What are some of the best research findings on augmented human intelligence?</u> (...)

Well, it may be difficult to verify this scientifically, but some of these results may be important:

STEP 1

A Theory of 128 best ideas was constructed which seemed cyclical and therefore complete. This method included general logical ideas like exponential efficiency and calculus. However, this theory was not much focused on specific physical inventions <u>The Power System Ideas Catalog</u>

STEP 2

With <u>Radical Ideas List</u> the ideas were shrunk to 32, but more focused on major categories of genius somewhat like communication and a theory of everything.

STEP 3

# THE GLASS OF EDUCATION

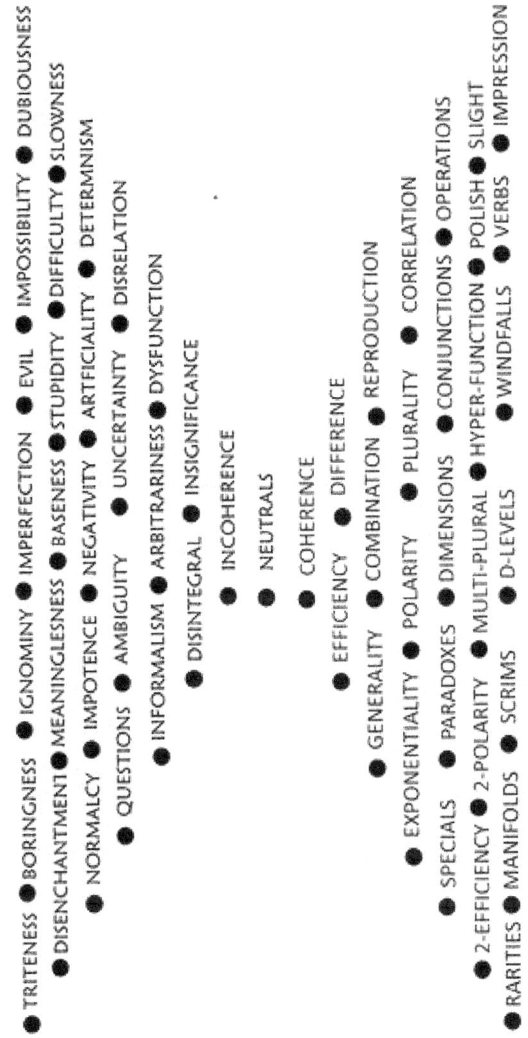

Based on category theory, a pyramid structure was formed which comprises the lower section of the hourglass. This pyramid included 28 categories, however, when the Radical Ideas was consulted, eight of them were found to be duplicates. This left 20 remaining ideas. Meanwhile, I had found mathematical evidence that 20 ideas was the archetypal number for a genius, which became more cemented when I noticed that a spectrum of opposites might be represented by two inventions, and applying polymathy would mean X10 equals 20 total great inventions. These types of equations were tried many times, with the end result seeming to never be below exactly 20 when full variety was considered. Cognitive models, lists of categories of human historical inventions, and theory of everything categories were tried to this end. For example, when the 25 major categories of the TOE were considered, it was determined that six categories had to do with impossibility, thus when the general category of impossibility was added to the remaining categories the result was still 20. The evidence seemed overwhelming that in a broad strokes sense, 20 categories was exactly right. The systems being considered were far above the average as far as understanding reality and ingenuity.

STEP 4

The greatest works of every major known philosopher and inventor were considered associatively to determine similarities between first, second, third... 20th major works, with the theory that when it came to the greatest inventions, few inventors or philosophers really had even 10 major works. When this process was taken to 20 items, it seemed to have a sense of possible completeness, and the items in the list had the following properties when constructed for an excel file. It was later thought this could be the basis for an intelligence or personality model.

GREAT PHILOSOPHY HISTORICAL MODEL BY NATHAN COPPEDGE

What is obvious (about the person)? [input]

What is the opposite of the thing that was obvious (previous)? [input]

What is trivial in this time in history? [input]

Pathetic argument that might win for this person? [input]

What is the better 2-step (re-do) of [trivial]?

WISE ANSWER? [input]

What is most required for [trivial]???

You will find it is [WISE ANSWER]

PRIMARY INVENTION [WISE ANSWER]

That wishes for [trivial]

MAJOR WORK 1: [Opposite of obvious] application of [WISE ANSWER].

MAJOR WORK 2: Theory missing [trivial]

MAJOR WORK 3: In more than one way [trivial] is [obvious]

MAJOR WORK 4: [trivial] is also [opposite of obvious]

MAJOR WORK 5: [obvious] IT IS... BUT IT IS ALSO [opposite of obvious]

MAJOR WORK 6: Variations on concepts of [trivial]

MAJOR WORK 7: Theories about theory missing [trivial]

MAJOR WORK 8: [Opp of obvious] is missing something!

MAJOR WORK 9: Not [Obvious] with [Wise answer]

MAJOR WORK 10: [Wise answer] is great

MAJOR WORK 11: Wishing for [Trivial] is not [Obvious]

MAJOR WORK 12: What is not [Obvious] is [Wise answer]

MAJOR WORK 13: [Trivial] is missing, a theory missing [Trivial]

MAJOR WORK 14: A theory of [Trivial] is not a theory

MAJOR WORK 15: [Trivial] beyond [Trivial] beyond [Trivial]

MAJOR WORK 16: Beyond [Trivial] IS [Opp of Obvious]

MAJOR WORK 17: Paradoxical [Opp of Obvious]

MAJOR WORK 18: [Trivial] IS paradoxical

MAJOR WORK 19: Paradoxical [Obvious]

MAJOR WORK 20: [Wise answer] transcends reality

Philosopher is remembered as studying [Opposite of obvious]

—<u>What did you do that you think was very creative?</u> (...)

...

STEP 5

These psychological patterns were then observed in the '20 Major Works' for all philosophers and inventors:

Major Accomplishment 1 is exceptional for a paradoxical genius.

Major Accomplishments 2 - 8 are shared between paradoxical geniuses and idiots unless the paradoxical genius has a better concept of what is trivial.

Major Accomplishments 9 and 10 always benefit by genius or paradoxical genius.

Major Accomplishments 11 to 15 benefit by concepts and knowing what is trivial, and potentially also using contrasts.

Major Accomplishments 16 to 19 benefit by being a bad person.

Major Accomplishment 20 benefits only by being a genius except at the cost of sanity. Normalcy is rewarded with sanity.

—<u>Theory of Intelligent Accomplishments</u> (...)

...

- <u>Experiences of Consciousness</u> (...)

A KIND OF PERSONAL HISTORY OF CONSCIOUSNESS

I will give you a record of my most conscious moments that I remember between 7 Million BC and 2021 AD. In theory this could serve to explain some modes of consciousness, in how they develop. This assumes an American consumer is more advanced than most of these in some cases or that particular compromises are necessary for higher dimensions or greater sensations:

In 7 Million BC I was a perfect being who could exist in two dimensions, called the Oroboros. He was accused of not knowing of sensation. [FALL FROM WISDOM]

7 Million BC I then became a red spinosaurus taken to be a dragon, who ate a child and then was punished with the spell 'wither and forget'. [GUILT]

In 6 Million BC I noticed very large, green eggs and seemingly drowned in them. Like green eggs and ham without the ham. [SENSATION]

I became reincarnated as 'The Draconian' a being who could survive in outer space who may have invented art, maps, and metaphysics. [PRODIGY]

In 1,000,000 BC I created a very loud noise which seemed to echo across the universe. [INTENT TO KILL]

In 100,000 BC I consulted a goddess and decided meaning and souls were good ideas. [INTELLECTUAL]

In 70,000 BC I traveled to the city of Ur and invented time-travel with Aristotle. [MAGIC]

In 40,000 BC I directed an army of men who were instructed to act like pigs in their first battle. [LEADERSHIP]

In 11,000 BC I was pegged as a Sumerian writer and transcended in the logos. [EXCEPTIONAL ABILITY]

In 9,000 BC I made coins at my father's forge and created the first martial art. I also conquered the world, met the gods, made a flower wilt with my mind, and slept in the house of my dead friend. [DIVINITY, MONEY, GUILT]

In 7,000 BC I saw the breasts of Isis, named Horus, bought the Souls of 3 Men, Told the tale of the 3 Monsters of History, blew crap into outer space, and was admonished on my stupidity. [UNFINISHED BUSINESS, DIVINITY, GUILT, BLAME]

In 0 AD I confabulated with a friend at Alexandria, covering over our crime with the story of Jesus of Nazareth. [MACHIAVELLIANISM, CRIME]

In 200 AD I was mutilated, and then gambled with men, and my head was cut off when I was pregnant and I was thrown in the ocean. [INDULGENCE, PUNISHMENT]

In 1000 AD I solved an unsolvable riddle thereby inventing the decimal system, killed 9 men and my wife, and invented the concept of suicide by telling a friend to kill me and then call my death lucky after I was gone. [CRIME AND PUNISHMENT]

Later, I was a boy who fell from a tower and invented Tarot. I was supposed to watch over my Dad the paranoid mercenary. I broke my leg trying to impress a prostitute and was so in love I could melt the snow. [TOUGHNESS, PAIN, AND BRILLIANCE]

In 1515 - 1540 my father was very wealthy, I thought babies could swallow diamonds and drink them like water. I had a sensation of growing very large breasts while I was on a boat headed to England. I tasted a sweet plum and I had an orgasm with a cart driver. I loved children who loved bakers and invented words on a piece of stolen parchment. [WOMANLY INDULGENCE, DIED YOUNG]

In 1777 to 1799 or so I visited witches to seal my wish for perpetual motion machines. Later I was on cocaine and invented the word 'neoeon'. Everyone thought I was the devil, and they cut off my head. [CONCEALED GENIUS, CRIME AND PUNISHMENT]

In 1790 - 1870 or so, I rewrote a check for 1000 times what it was worth thereby securing the future of the United States. I acted like a god of war to destroy the Pueblo Indians and retired with a witch who wanted to send me to hell. I tried to remember how to time-travel, but things grew cloudy. [SUPERIORITY, LONG LIFE, WISDOM AND MEMORY]

In 1830 or so I was an idiot who wanted to eat hamburgers. I could taste food in my mouth finally. Ketchup maybe. I thought I had invented Orfin An and on my deathbed I decided I wanted to be a self-named orphan in my next life. [INDULGENCE, FOOLISHNESS, MEDIOCRITY]

In 1860 or so I wanted to be the town doctor, and made a big campaign. All I could arrange was to be a proctologist. I was the famous Rip Van Winkl. When we were conscripted for the South I said we should surrender because we had no weapons, which was true enough. I had to steel things to survive along the railroad tracks, I was in pain from swallowing nails because I was hungry, and tried to take drugs. I saw my perfect family, and died of Jews dancing the lambada which made me feel like a coward. [EGO, TOUGHNESS, DISAPPOINTMENT]

I became Euler or Eulucipher, whose life was a double-lie. He couldn't remember being guilty. He lived rationally his whole life, God wrote his books, and he gave away his wife. He was a spy for America, and ended up hooked up on drugs. He died of infinity and nightmares, the two numbers. [EFFORT, GENIUS, COMPROMISE]

Then I fell. I became an abortion clinic assistant who traveled the world until he ended up in Germany. He would interpret people being exterminated. He was shot and tried to sell his soul. Then he sang the Song of Life. Secretly he was a 7 million year old Oroboros. [SELF-DECEIT, EVIL, MEANING OF LIFE]

Then I was captured by America. They told me I would experience pain forever. I might as well work on ideas. I thought of the phrase 'Ah, Googlie' and trillionaires. People seemed to have trouble thinking. [EFFORT, GUILT, EARNESTY]

Then I became Nathan Coppedge.

When I was 3 years old, I looked at particular metal clothes lines used for drying clothes as symbols of archetypal machines which showed a hidden level of reality. I also thought that the gas meters for heating the apartment were really for narcotic drugs. [CONCEALED GUILT, DELUSION, FEAR]

When I was 10 I hurt myself falling off a canoe said I 'teeened' my teeth on the side of the canoe as a way to remember my invention, the perpetual motion rotor boat. This invention later led to my development of inventions on perpetual motion machines. [UNCONSCIOUS GUILT, PUNISHMENT]

In 2000, I achieved the Jung "Eye Stage" at age 18, which according to a psychologist is not particularly late or early. I was watching a Chinese girl who was my friend, walking with her umbrella in the rain. [INFLATED EGO, HUMILITY, COMPROMISE]

In 2000 I decided it was the last possibility of perpetual motion becoming possible. So, I put together some toys, and the principle was brilliant but no one would believe me. [RECOVERED GENIUS, PARTIAL MESSIAH COMPLEX, PARIAHISM]

In 2004 I decided I would eat fish as a way of improving my brain. [ADMISSION OF GUILT, COMPROMISE, SELF-DECEIT]

In 2005 I discovered that a coin could theoretically roll with a higher midpoint after one turn than it's base on the previous turn, supporting the principle of perpetual motion. We were at a coin swallower machine at Mystic Seaport. [NEW IDEAS, INTELLIGENCE]

In 2013 I uncovered a method of categorical knowledge which could serve as the basis of coherence theory, and improved a method on perpetual motion machines. [REALITY, BRILLIANCE, COMPROMISE]

In 2015 I gained insights into mathematical limits. [OLD IDEAS, HUMILITY]

At the end of 2016 I learned about short Socratic lectures. [OLD IDEAS, BRILLIANCE, CAFFEINE ADDICTION]

In 2017 I decided my formula for souls was right. I had considered it for about one year. [CARE, DESIRE, REWARD]

In 2018 I learned about Chinese writing. [CONNEXIONS, HUMILITY, BRILLIANCE]

In May 2019 I thought of perpetual motion flying machines. [HIGHER MIND, INTELLIGENCE, CATEGORIES]

- Nirvana might help in odd moments (like a bug with sensitive feelers with M.C. Escher: meaning theory of consciousness).
- Psychopaths might have serendipity: EVOLUTION OF GENETIC INTELLIGENCE: Humility --
> Sacrosanctitudes --> Animal Intelligence --> Writ of Serendipity --
> Disorganization --
> Antiquarianism --> Carnivorism --
> Spawns and Spawning
- People who close their eyes when they are talking are probably not masochists.
- Irrationalists may not have thought of the concept of 'irrational disorder' early enough.
- Valerie Solanas might be diagnosed with some kind of 'broken oven syndrome' or perhaps she's just sort of a vigilante.
- Who overdoses on salt? The people that overdo it on salt of course, because it's measured against zero.
- Crystals: Potentially worth money because you will always have crystals in your life (they are 4-dimensional), but otherwise, not much. Maybe

more dreaming or less, or fewer nightmares, but not a big effect.

- The chemical in soccer cleats (knobbed shoes) may cause anger problems.
- You might like to analyze the name Nathan Larkin Coppedge and what it means. I have never heard a convincing argument that name analysis is 100% inaccurate. You think if your name was Hickory it would have nothing to do with wood or trees? I think you would find that is inaccurate. Now you might say Linden is a tree, so you might think I'm a stupid person. Possibly I seem stupid, but if you believe that is because I have the middle name of a tree, you should also have a high probability of believing I look like an engineer in some way. If I don't look like an engineer, but other Larkins do look like engineers, then it is likely there is something enginery about me that has to do with 'Nathan' and 'Coppedge'. It's a basic argument to get that far (a lot of Larkins do look like Larkins, that is beyond probability), but if you go further you

may find some interesting things about me.

- Case examples of psychotropic meds using roleplaying stats: Mental Health: 5 / 20 (40 / 100) Paranoid schizophrenia +3 with medication. [8 mg resperidone per day will provide +4, 6 mg will provide +3].
- How does Nathan Coppedge react to a sip of espresso? Nathan didn't try this on purpose. He avoided coffee drinks until he was around his 40s or beyond. While Nathan found the espresso sample increased his energy relative to two or three large chai teas, his productivity did not immediately increase, and the effect was zero so far on his rate of inventing. It is thought to be more a difference of energy than intelligence. I concluded I shouldn't try more because it always causes burnout.

OBJECTIVE EDUCATION LIFE CYCLE

-4-D [PURPOSEFUL] DIFFERENT POEM -->
-3-D [BEAUTIFUL] CATEGORICAL VIGNETTE -->
-2-D [PERSONAL] PSYCHOLOGICAL GILT -->
-1-D [ORIGINAL] PHILOSOPHICAL LITERATURE -->

2-D [WRITERS] LANGUAGE BOOK -->
4-D [POETRY] POWER ORGANIZATION -->
6-D [UPSHOT OF HISTORY] UNIQUE PERFECTION -->
11-D [ARTWORKS] PARADOXICAL DIMENSION -->

10-D [GREAT AMBITIONS] WISHING FOR MAGIC -->
9-D [WEIGHING ALTERNATIVES] THEORY BASICS -->
8-D [CONSIDERING EXCEPTIONS] CYCLICAL DIALECTIC -->
7-D [MATCHING CATEGORIES] UNIVERSAL SCIENCE -->

5-D [EXPONENTIAL EFFICIENCY] EX: DIAGRAM OF OMNISCIENCE -->
3-D [VAR 1: MODULARITY] EX: ETERNAL ENERGY -->
1-D [VAR 2: INDIVIDUALISM] EX: EVOLUTIONARY CURRENTS -->
-5-D [IMMACULATE EQUATION] EX: EFFICIENCY + DIFFERENCE -->

-4-D... -->

## CASE STUDY: POSSIBILITY OF SIN

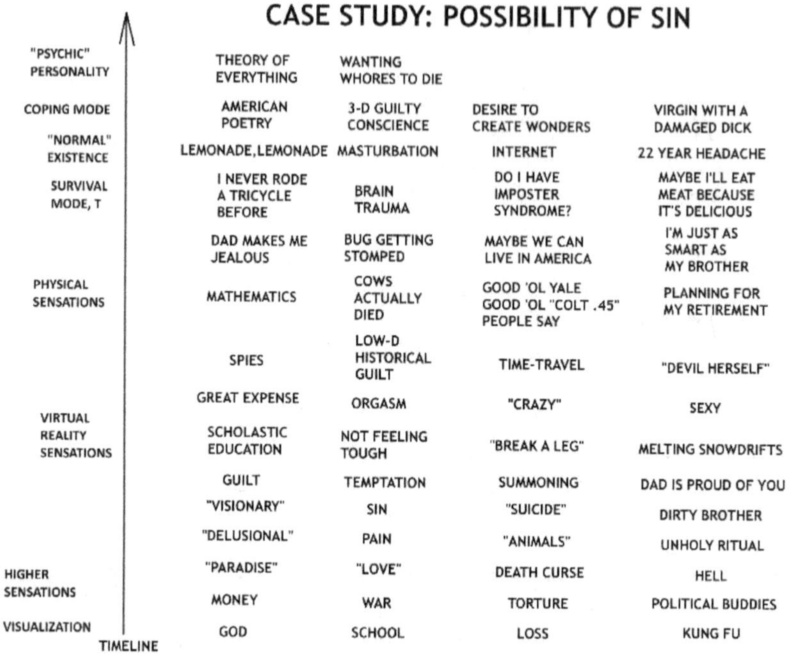

|  | | | | |
| --- | --- | --- | --- | --- |
| "PSYCHIC" PERSONALITY | THEORY OF EVERYTHING | WANTING WHORES TO DIE | | |
| COPING MODE | AMERICAN POETRY | 3-D GUILTY CONSCIENCE | DESIRE TO CREATE WONDERS | VIRGIN WITH A DAMAGED DICK |
| "NORMAL" EXISTENCE | LEMONADE,LEMONADE | MASTURBATION | INTERNET | 22 YEAR HEADACHE |
| SURVIVAL MODE, T | I NEVER RODE A TRICYCLE BEFORE | BRAIN TRAUMA | DO I HAVE IMPOSTER SYNDROME? | MAYBE I'LL EAT MEAT BECAUSE IT'S DELICIOUS |
| | DAD MAKES ME JEALOUS | BUG GETTING STOMPED | MAYBE WE CAN LIVE IN AMERICA | I'M JUST AS SMART AS MY BROTHER |
| PHYSICAL SENSATIONS | MATHEMATICS | COWS ACTUALLY DIED | GOOD 'OL YALE GOOD 'OL "COLT .45" PEOPLE SAY | PLANNING FOR MY RETIREMENT |
| | SPIES | LOW-D HISTORICAL GUILT | TIME-TRAVEL | "DEVIL HERSELF" |
| | GREAT EXPENSE | ORGASM | "CRAZY" | SEXY |
| VIRTUAL REALITY SENSATIONS | SCHOLASTIC EDUCATION | NOT FEELING TOUGH | "BREAK A LEG" | MELTING SNOWDRIFTS |
| | GUILT | TEMPTATION | SUMMONING | DAD IS PROUD OF YOU |
| | "VISIONARY" | SIN | "SUICIDE" | DIRTY BROTHER |
| | "DELUSIONAL" | PAIN | "ANIMALS" | UNHOLY RITUAL |
| HIGHER SENSATIONS | "PARADISE" | "LOVE" | DEATH CURSE | HELL |
| | MONEY | WAR | TORTURE | POLITICAL BUDDIES |
| VISUALIZATION | GOD | SCHOOL | LOSS | KUNG FU |

TIMELINE

<u>Case Study: Person Who Might Think They're a Fool:</u>

Do I know that I don't know? has been a tough question for me recently.

Most professional academics would answer, 'no, Nathan doesn't know that he doesn't know, because he's not very wise.'

I am not sure, but the question makes me feel a bit foolish.

It can be a pretense to say that I'm not a pretender at wisdom, but it can also be a pretense to be a pretender. Thus, there don't seem to be a lot of good options.

Nietzsche was very outspoken against having pretenses, saying it was the most important thing to avoid them. On the other hand, it is not always certain if Nietzsche's judgment is absolute, some may think it is, or it may be past some time after the Greeks, but I am not sure.

I think I have had perspectives on pretenses too, but I realize a lot of it is borrowed from Nietzsche, some of the poetry may not be his though.

I have perspectives on irrationality that point towards post-irrationality as the only rationality. This smacks of being simply inside the land of opinion, but I think it may be deeper. The knowledge systems I have created or thought to have created since writing on post-irrationality seem to do something useful with the irrational concept, making it seem worthwhile.

I don't want to sacrifice what I've worked on because it looks like there's no alternative. I don't think I'm painted into a corner of knowledge, but I may sometimes still feel like someone engaging in folly.

I have tried to trump folly by making very practical inventions, but I think inventors and philosophers alike are fallible human beings and it would be difficult to defend absolute wisdom without either living a virtuous life where one didn't end up depressed, or a life in which one has thought of every possible invention.

Since the human appetite is insatiable, these other options from folly don't look real.

So, I turn back to locate what I meant by foolishness, and end up feeling I have a lot of knowledge that is worthwhile. But I still look like a fool, so that is confusing. Maybe my wisdom is far from absolute, or maybe I did something wrong, or some combination. It seems to me half the time someone looks like a fool they have not even committed any major sin. But the other half I would hope to have a defense against being someone who led a worthless life and didn't even believe anything. I think I have beliefs, and I'm not sure I've done the worst things, but since I'm branded a fool I realize things could look very bad even if I didn't do anything bad. That makes me feel out of touch with my skin.

Futuristic Research: Having an offline objective interface using simple Nathan Coppedge heuristics might be interesting. There might be a cult following in adapting objective interfaces to every type of personality characteristic.
Poisonous mushrooms might kill brain cells.

Do nose-pickers resist Lyme disease? Wondering. I pick my nose frequently, and my score in Lyme antibodies is 0.18 (supposedly low is good because it means not having been bitten by a tick carrying the virus. My brother and sister both had Lyme disease, and neither of them picks their nose frequently).

Marriage has been said to lead to longer life, but only for the woman if she survives childbirth, and for the man if they stay married.

Socializing has sometimes been associated with the probability of harmful addictive behaviors and with dependent relationships, but not always. A tenuous connection has also been drawn to depression in certain personalities, but this has probably been ignored due to assumptions bias.

I would like to see results of beneficial effects over time on people who are completely un-frustrated, and who test high in sensitivity, and who are not taking a narcotic, and who did not suffer from child abuse, were never depressed, are not lying, and do not die before age 79.

Maybe Apatosaurs or Brontosaurs have variation from birth.

Would the <u>Casimir Effect</u> really exist on Mars, or does it just exist with an Earth atmosphere?

The next step, unless you adopt a very broad and useless definition, is to abandon it, because it hit a dead end with the Casimir Effect.

Although the Casimir Effect does exist, and it does have nifty properties, it has been labeled a form of zero-point energy, which is probably not what it is, because the effect disappears when the metal surfaces move, and it can even disappear gradually over time. I have even suspected it may be a function of air pressure not it's own effect at all. Would the Casimir Effect really exist on Mars, or does it just exist with an Earth atmosphere? And does the effect actually function like magnetism at all, or does it just prevent surfaces from contacting quickly? Maybe the Casimir Effect is really maggots?

Instead, you should investigate very clever yet traditional mechanical principles, specifically those investigated by Nathan Coppedge since 2006 (I didn't really do any experiments until 2009, and my first sign of successful over-unity was in Nov 2013, less than 5 years ago)


Philosophy as a Symptom of an Abortive Society (...)

2022–02–04

Between 1610 and 1709 questions were transcendental, 'Was he mede like black folk?', 'Is she soo much womane?', 'That is like a childe to me'.

Between 1710 and 1809 questions were concerns of faith, such as: 'Have I sinned?', 'Have I been true to my vows?' and 'Are you quite certain?'. Some of it was also like 'Are there any living savages left?' and 'Can I break you?'

Between 1810 and 1909 questions were not as common as later, but some of them were 'Is drink the devils sin?', 'Am I right in the head?' and 'Am I enough of a man?'

Between 1910 and 2016 the most common question was probably 'Why?' or existential questions such as 'What is existence?' and 'What is reality?' and 'Is there a God?'

<u>Socially-Enforced Hypochondriacs?</u> (...)

Case 1: FAKE IMPOSTER SYNDROME: Who's the first person you remember arguing with and why?

I argued with a little boy in Venezuela. He said they were not my parents, they were his parents. My dad's conclusion was he was just angry that he did not get to move to America.

Sometimes I wonder if I have imposter syndrome, but this is probably because there was a boy later when we got back to the U.S. who pretended to be me in a photograph, but it was really a lookalike.

Case 2: AUG 2022 I REALIZED I HAVE A PROBLEM:

Relatives have been noticing a 'thing' on my back, which I was not able to see in the mirror. I went to the hospital years ago to investigate odd health symptoms and couldn't get a straight answer. It's like they recommended surgery because of 'something filling up my stomach' but they were speaking so softly I didn't know what they were talking about. It sounded like they meant something deadly but I couldn't tell what they meant. Years later my Dad was talking about how he would probably not attend my graduation, and my brother was talking about how I would be 'dead' but I had no idea what they were talking about because I still had not seen the 'thing' in the mirror. In August 2022 I finally observed it after I lost some weight, and it indeed looks something like a gigantic worm which possibly occupies a larger part of my inner organs by now. I am hoping there is still a cure that does not involve losing brain function. But I am worried that health treatments may result in death, which is something I don't want to happen. Meanwhile, I don't require much food, and my health seems pretty okay on the surface considering my passive lifestyle so this makes me wonder what I should do. Possibly I just did not understand the doctors when they asked if I should get X-rays because I was worried I was getting diagnosed with cancer.

"Emotional support and encouragement if desired may be directed by Quora message."

On the other hand, I have also had the feeling that my body is definitely doing something cool, and if I have a chance at immortality then my body will probably do something radical which could look a bit like having a worm on the surface to those who are not accustomed to bodies metamorphosizing. There is also the detail that my dead grandfather's work with nuclear energy may have caused some mutations in my body possibly including a double-throat and a long useless extra tube that flows through odd places in my body. Maybe the worm is extraneous to these various other oddities? I don't know how to find out other than letting the condition somehow get worse. But maybe the worm just isn't affecting my brain yet.

Another detail is that surgery might involve ripping up a lot of flesh, and would be painful, someone said. But I've been in pain before and I don't now how painful they mean.

I have been through a lot of oddities because of this unknown parasite. One of them was my dad chanting to me: "Pray that it's symbiotic". But it seemed sort of like a trick question.

But now I looked in the mirror and the worm seems to be gone, or consist of rug burns. So, I don't know what to think, I find this very confusing. Maybe I just have more basic health problems.

<u>Bedwetting</u> (...)

I think it translates as 'atta he'. But I am not sure of the specific meaning. Maybe dirty mouth or beer tosser or lonely old man or maybe empty case or someone who needs help or pees on themselves? It could possibly mean someone with a weak bladder (this isn't connected with 'weak blood': it means someone has a tendency to urinate on themselves without meaning to, for example, when they are asleep, or when they drink too much).

In the United States having a weak bladder is sometimes connected with a childhood disorder called 'bedwetting' that is connected with having a weak bladder or low self-confidence. Someone who chronically wets the bed is called a 'bedwetter'. It is more common in younger children, but sometimes can occur later in childhood, and usually goes away long before someone turns 18 unless the person is socially immature.

If someone wets the bed it is important to provide dry bedclothing every day or the person can become infected. If the person is somewhat older than about 7, or depending on maturity, the person should be gently told that bedwetting is not normal, and they won't ever be considered a grown up if they keep wetting the bed.

There are special plastic sheetings people can buy that will prevent most of the damage to a mattress. These plastic sheets can be washed simply by wiping them down with soap and water and drying them. Usually they have cotton / polyester coverings on top to make them more comfortable, but the top cover has to be washed unless you get tired of dealing with the problem. Still, if you don't give the child a chance to use normal bedclothes, they may sometimes become too tolerant of their own problem. Still, as long as the problem goes on you will probably want multiple sets of sheets and bed dressings so that the person does not smell bad during the day, and so that the person does not develop mold and sores on their body. If you scold your child too much or if the child develops sores, you may be blames for being a neglectful parent, and the child may even be taken away to a foster home or an orphanage. You could also have criminal penalties. So, it is best to treat the child like they are your own even if they have a bedwetting problem.

Another thing to keep in mind is bedwetters usually don't do it intentionally. It usually happens during the night while they are asleep, or because they can't hold the grape juice in their bladder or whatever. If you give them kind instructions and offer them hope, the bedwetting usually goes away in a few years, or in rare cases immediately. There is hope for improvement unless the person is socially immature, however, it takes kind words and encouragement. If the child gets too angry they may try to take revenge by 'peeing everywhere' even though originally it was unintentional. So, try to be nice. It often takes time, because their bladder is weak, often because of a combination of physical and psychological factors. In fact, bedwetting can be a sign that parents need to pay attention and start caring about their child. The child may be unconsciously complaining about how they are not getting the preferred treatment. It could be the child needs more treats or more responsibility before they are likely to improve all the way. It could be the mother still thinks the child is a baby, and the child asserts what little power it has by expressing the child version of masculinity, which is to have some hard to manage symptoms. Remember it is not intentional, and you can't assume it will always happen unless you're just not caring for the child, or if the child is immature. Hurting the child's confidence is the worst thing you can do, and may have permanent consequences.

Keep in mind, the child may grow up to be someone pretty functional. It is usually just a phase and doesn't usually mean they will be like that as an adult. Sometimes resisting bedwetting can be predicted by how well the child does in school. If they do really well in school they have a pretty good chance of recovering within a year or two. This is because self-confidence is a factor, and controlling the bladder can actually be quite difficult for someone with a weak bladder. It's important not to focus on it because it's not intentional. Just tell them it's important and you want them to be mature like a grown up. Eventually the problem will probably go away. There's not much to do. Scolding them too much can degrade their self-esteem and actually make the problem much worse or even permanent. Many of the worst adult cases are people that just gave up because their parents were unchangeable and did not provide enough emotional support. Their parents didn't care is the main problem with bedwetting. It's not only hard for the child to figure out, it's also hard for the parent to figure out.

Another thing you can do is make the person wear a plastic diaper-type thing when they go to bed, but not during the day. You can tell them they have to wear it when they go to sleep until they stop wetting the bed. You can remind them they might feel embarrassed wearing a diaper and maybe they will eventually learn that they can control their bladder better. Making them wear it too much though might make them give up, so you have to give them a chance to try 'life without a diaper' sometimes or they may revert to babyhood. Making someone wear a diaper-thing more than a few times can be oppressive to someone's ego and functionality. So, if the person has a chance of recovering just by changing the sheets you should give them a chance so they don't just think they're a baby for the rest of their lives. To fight the tendency, it is important to say that you are 'worried' and that you 'care about their behavior'.

If the person is older than 18 bedwetting is probably connected with alcoholism or mental retardation or some type of diagnosable bladder problem perhaps more serious than bedwetting. In some cases that may be considered a different disorder it could be the person pees intentionally and has some type of fascination with urinating such as a belief that they are a dog, or a belief that they are always peeing on electric lines, or something else similarly bizarre. Usually though, in almost every case, bedwetting is a bladder and confidence problem unless the person is not mentally developed. You shouldn't assume the person is retarded unless they have always been far behind their peers in school, which is not usually true for a lot of students. Even students who get C's and D's sometimes are just faced with hard courses. You need to watch more closely if someone is considered socially immature or if they are permanently placed in classes for slow or disabled students. If the problem is just bladder or confidence, mental maturity may not be the concern, so much as how they feel about their family or their sense of what they are getting out of life.

It can be important to tell them: It's not the end of the world. But it can be very inconvenient for you, and it can be inconvenient for your parents. You don't want the kid on the knife's edge thinking they're going to die, but you want them to understand that although the world won't end it's still much better for the parents if you don't wet the bed. The kids basically know it would be better for themselves, but it's really quantumly complicated. They want to feel better about themselves, but it's like metaphysics, it's stuff that's been psychologically hurting them since birth, they probably won't feel better until they're 40 or so (don't tell them that), but they understand probably that they need to stop urinating in like one month or five year or whatever, but the parents aren't usually making them feel better about their whole life.

It's important not to make their life about urination. They don't need to practice in a toilet, they need to improve their beliefs about themselves and the respect they get from other people. They also need to practice self-control to some degree, but it's not 100% easy.

<u>Physics of the Will</u>: With a certain mentality, free will can be realistically simulated. If we have control over the appearance of the mentality, we may have control over the appearance of the simulation. (February 7, 2019)

1. Discrete energy.
2. Categorical menu.
3. Full idea expression.
4. Emotional preferences.
5. Eventual change.
6. Immediate decisions.
7. Magical fluency.

UFO Syndrome:

*What does it mean when I'm constantly reminding myself that things are real?* "Can't believe things are so real? It could be a coping behavior for mental health issues, or it could just mean you can't believe how good / bad your life is. Or, with younger people, it could be you viewed work by Nathan Coppedge which seemingly contradicts science. Or, you could have trouble coping with evidence fake or not of UFO's." --<u>What does it mean when I'm constantly reminding myself that things are real?</u> (...)

Women: Get in touch with mint and potatoes. This is probably what women used to eat because they had knowledge of herbs. Men were foolish and ate bird meat. This explains why men now have a weight problem, since their hips are supposed to be narrow, while women do not gain as much weight.

SUMMATION AS SANTA CLAUS:

Sum --> Imprecision --> Santa Claus --> Situations --> Intelligence --> Rule-breaking --> (Sum). Humans may be fulfilling the role of Santa Claus when acting in history and performing science.

"You can simplify the interface by creating occasional subtle embarrassment to create blood circulation in their face, and by taking 'yes' and 'no' inputs from the user."—<u>What ideas are absolutely necessary in the next version of social media?</u>

...

Keep in mind, while those recognized as geniuses are often high achievers, it may be partly propaganda which ones are noticed.

1880's: doctors viewed as genius. 1910's: inventor of pennecillin viewed as genius.

1920's: master race viewed as genius. 1940's: winning battle viewed as genius.

1950's: Government is viewed as genius. 1970's: Government physicists viewed as masterminds.

1970's: Californians were viewed as geniuses. 1990's: Californians run technology.

1990's: Asians were viewed as smart. 2010 - 2020: An Asian is viewed as a greatest genius.

—<u>Are geniuses always a genius?</u> (...)

...

If you don't remember being born or being in the womb you probably have a poor memory, low self-awareness, low stimulation, or have a focus on instantly growing up, or did not experience trauma afterwards.

...

Connection between Criminalism and Genius:

4/20 great ideas benefit by breaking rules.

4/20 great ideas benefit by intelligence, paradox, and madness.

12/20 great ideas benefit by rules and triviality.

[How to cure criminality is either to make ethics work for these results or oppose intellectualism. However, another factor is reverse psychology, so actually exposing people to science or creativity could be a good strategy for opposing intellect].

—<u>Are high IQ people typically linear or non-linear thinkers?</u>

...

<u>Aesthetic Survival Manifesto</u> (…)

Originally July 5, 2020.

Thus, it could be summed 'philosophers win, the only thing deadly is a standard'. —Poetic Planning Updated principle: Some parts futuristic, some parts balanced, some parts symmetric.

Existentialists value things which stand out, like beauty, functionality, and innovation. Things which stand out represent a tough-as-would-have-it attitude towards survival aesthetics. Since what appears to survive is what survives, aesthetics is unavoidable. What stands out for survival is the aesthetic of survival, and when survival must appear to survive it is a survival aesthetic. What serves the survival aesthetic is what stands out, such as beauty, functionality, and innovation.

LATER NOTES:

WHY ART SURVIVES:

RULES SO FAR SUPPORT THE SURVIVAL OF ART:

I suppose you could search for 'art' to see if art is up or down.

Then search for 'modernism' to see if modern art is up or down.

Then if modern art is up, search 'abstract art' and see if abstract art is up or down.

If abstract art is up, search the key words searched under abstract art.

If abstract art is down, search 'photography' or 'photo-realism'.

Otherwise, if modern art is down, search 'impressionism' or 'abstract expressionism' to see if it is up or down.

If everything is down so far, most likely art is down, though you can try 'fringe artists' or 'boutique art' or 'furniture' and see if these are selling in spite of the rest.

If all of this is down, most likely music is up to exceptional highs or history is being very boring or very dangerous. However, such periods of boredom and danger seem exceptionally rare, so most likely music is up or one of the categories above is doing moderately well.

—Why Art Survives (...)


...

Qualia in Aesthetic Survival:

Pretty simple. Qualia are for the purposes of human psychology. They don't exist per se, but they are a legitimate form of translation, in that humans need a layer of softness in order to avoid damaging their own brain. This layer may be explained as emotionalism, or just suitability of information, or other niceties, depending on how the brain happens to be working. Avoiding niceties is possible but implies that someone wants to take damage.

We might gain weight from niceties, yet niceties is right where we are now. We just want more niceties is more likely that destroying them.

—If we were to calculate the brain atom by atom, what outcome would suggest that a considered system should have qualia?

## Planetary Stim Hypothesis

2021–02–25

(A) No drugs are present, there is no existential moment, and no interpretation.

(B) One drug is present, the drug is refined, dominant species has an existential moment, then species becomes dependent on the drug.

(C) Several drugs are present, several drugs are refined, the dominant species has an existential moment, and the species becomes dependent on several drugs.

(D) A drug species is dominant, the otber species feels existential anxiety and the less dominant species is eliminated by the drug-dependent species.

In case (D) if the drug dependent species varies it is easy to see that most species would die.

In cases (B) and (C), if we take the Formula for Extinction seriously, subspecies who focus on drugs to excess could be unnecessarily committed to s single trait, which generally spells extinction in sub-species.

However, the remaining case, Case (A) provides only for brute survival.

<u>Funny Intuition and Real Insanity</u>

FUNNY INTUITIONS

"2001–Y Yang says"—News of the Absurdly Wise and Mysterious

"Perpetual motion is literally the beginning of magic…" —Radical Ideas List (…)

"Someone needs to help their mother who doesn't know English with paperwork for citizenship, however, they are currently locked up as an insane case." — What are some real-life examples of paradoxical intention? (…)

REAL INSANITY (February 18, 2021)

The idea is that particular days in the numatic calendar, due to time and space, and subject to certain sublime fluctuations, are infinitely unique, and so they represent particular unique cornucopias.

I think I'll add a single paranthesis. Why? A better question is how?

I am resting on a different island, an impossible island.

Corners of invisible rooms.

Skip, madness, skip.

An Argument that Philosophers may be Useful

(Nov 19, 2020)

First of all, here are some results.

On Google Scholar, these people are known for what might be philosophical coherence:

https://scholar.google.com/citations?view_op=search_authors&hl=en&mauthors=label%3Acoherence_theory

These scientists are also known for the scientific end of
coherence: https://scholar.google.com/citations?hl=en&view_op=search_authors&mauthors=label%3Acoherence&btnG=

On Quora, these people are known for being Top 10 Writers in coherence:

https://www.quora.com/topic/Coherence/writers

Of these writers, few if any are writers with academic citations. Currently the number one writer on Quora in Coherence Theory is ME. I am also someone who has citations on coherence, but I am not #1 on Google Scholar. This leads me to believe that I am the ONLY writer on real academic coherence who is not writing about science.

Now, I have done an extensive search. If I list all of these scholars names, each individually with perfect spelling, after the term 'theory of everything'. What comes up? What is the net result?

HERE IS AN EXTENSIVE EVALUATION OF THE RESULTS FOUND:

Greg Gbur — Physicist with research on 'Falling Felines'.

Xi Chen — possibly mathematics

Nathan Coppedge —"The Theory of Everything" philosophical theory, extensive materials.

Emil Wolf —- Pioneer in optics, now deceased, widely cited.

Garth Williams —Illustrated Charlotte's Web.

David ATTWOOD— Seems to be an expert on ultraviolet radiation.

Maxim S. Pshenichnikov — Coulomb effect, nanodefraction, spectroscopy. Few results.

Domenico Pacifici — "fundamental property of light".

Pierre Thibault — conceptual artist / architect known for quaint minimalism.

David R. Mandel —Canadian defense agency, counterfactualism.

Jeremy Dahl — "creative mind" with his wife, hiearchical address book...

Yanwei Liu — X-ray microscopy "I hope everything is going well".

Jesse N. Clark — Elliptically bent X-ray nanomaterials... Few results.

Aeron Tynes Hammack— Locus biosciences. Dual-beam laser traps.

Sid JA Hubbard—Operators in strongly correlated electrons.

Lauren J. Human —Utilizing trait observability to disentangle judgeability

Dina Carbone — Nanofibers. Few results.

Yin Song — Neuroimaging, data science lab. Not many results.

Rakesh kumar Singh—Air Marshal.

Sebastian Roling—Photonics or something. Not many results.

Naresh Satyan—Semiconductor optics, comets.

Oscar G. Rodríguez-Herrera—Catodioptric parallel processors.

Mikhaël Myara — acronyms about photonics.

Bo Chen — physical dynamics, estimation theory, query processing.

Zhengyun Zhang — mathematics, light field.

Dr Bartlomiej Siwicki — phase coherence, biocompatible.

Yobani Mejia — BA in biochemistry, at Arizona State otherwise little information.

Oleg Gorobtsov— coherent synchrotron.

Tiberiu Tudor—Mueller matrix algrebra, polarimetry.

Doug Renshaw—Biomechanics, Tasmanian fire service.

Dominique Derauw —Advisory committee for stability of Antarctic ice shelves.

Arpit Joshi—multiprocessor software design, parallel algorithms, intel.

Vinu RV—optical imaging through complex scattering.

Youyou Hu — nutrition book.

Lara McManus —catholic school, sorority.

Simon Brezan— Biological coherence.

Francisco García-Rosales—conference of neuroethology.

Madara Lakshika Marasinghe—vortex networks.

Matthew R. Morgan—Wittgenstein, Wittgenstein, arguments for God's existence.

JunWoo Kim—inventor of a coin-collecting cryptocurrency.

Heath Gemar—graduate student at NASA? Not many results.

Magnus Norgren— "chelating agents" in metal, bubble formation.

Abhinandan Bhattacharjee—quantum physics, go barefoot.

Suchita—finance or dark matter formation.

izuchukwu udochi nwachukwu—"Direct Mapped Caches" maybe African?

Darshika Singh—free trade, Soho.

George Papademetriou—exorcism, possibly ordained priest.

Jungeun Choi—shamanism, book design.

Arvind Yelashetty—No real results, name partly matches an actor from a movie about TOEs.

CB Singh—Handbook of seed testing. "Seed testing is performed in dedicated laboratories by trained and usually certified analysts... The various classes of improved seeds are recognized to facilitate the maintenance of genetic purity of the variety and to ensure a continuous supply of good quality seed at a reasonable cost."

Jesse Raffield— masters degree in physics, perhaps wrongly associated with Hawking's TOE book.

Christy Moseley—knows about coherence in English papers.

Marvin Glover—Yin-yang, Max Tegmark, not many results.

Mark John Fernee—Australian physicist.

Tipper Rumpf—EMLab mold sampling mentor.

Bill Otto—nuclear missile engineer.

Keith Ramsay—Homeland security, "makes everything easier", critiqued by a mathematician.

Mahesh Prakash— "combining digital terrain and surface textures".

Quinn Rusnell—advocate for constructive experimental philosophy He believes "it's far fetched to expect a theory of everything if 'everything' is understood [to mean absolutely everything in knowledge]"

Bob Guenther—encyclopedia of modern optics.

John Rodrigues—possibly a bishop, speaker on dyslexia.

...

Now here is why you might value a philosopher on the topic of something obscure which relates to logic! Notice I am really the only useful name here for real coherence in philosophy, or whoever it is either doesn't list coherence in their Academia credentials or is not a top writer in Coherence on Quora.

From this we can discern:

- Scientific experts do not yet use 'coherence' to refer to a Theory of Everything, over seven years after Nathan's book on coherent philosophy was published.
- There are no major experts in 'traditional coherence' because it was not known terminology.

## (CONTINUED CASE STUDY ON VALUING PHILOSOPHERS):

Just a little "caution" about the concept of inventor-scientist, basically it's two words:

Of the top 50 most prolific inventors and polymaths counting only great inventions, only 8 / 50 that I have found are major Western scientists, one of them being Nazi Germany and one being Francis Galton. A few more are Asian and not always scientists, but most are either artists, philosophers, or polymaths of some type who are not known to be scientists at all or who are known mostly for philosophy or entertainment.

There are a number of scientists in the overall list however, they are not necessarily the majority or always the most educated of the scientists who make discoveries.

Quite a few contributors are simply pioneering within some type of manufacturing or simply thought of a casual idea on a whim, or were inspired by some type of practical method like stopping bullets or cleaning dishes.

The top performers very often simply come up with a list of new words, or in some cases they contribute to whole new categories of invention which they have some claim to inventing themselves, sort of like if Einstein had gone on to build a time-machine, a teleporter, and faster-than-light travel, except doing most of it from the living room. Many of the top inventors leave the practical application up to other people, but the best of them may have a list of 11 or more major ideas.

Once you get a knack for it, it's easy to climb the list. It helps to know the list exists and to compare yourself with some of the other inventors. Some of the inventions are very casual, they just have to be big ideas that no one else thought of that could mean something intellectually or practically.

The Greatest Inventors.

(CONTINUED CASE STUDY ON VALUING PHILOSOPHERS): HOW DO WE KNOW WHEN WE KNOW SOMETHING?

Why metaphysics may be helpful in avoiding blue blow pops.

1. Similarity, like 1 + 1.

2. Grasping, like I can estimate that if I offer $1 million the bully will not destroy my Dad's car.

3. Familiarity, like I just would not believe my mother would ever do that.

4. Habit, like I have done these problems before, they're not that difficult.

5. Experience, like I can guess the gas station is still there because I've always used it to navigate on my way home. At least if it's gone I'll know it's gone.

6. Wisdom, like although blue blow-pops may look delicious, I know the blue dye does nothing good for my circulatory system.

7. Understanding, like I could taste a blue blow-pop in my mind if I want to, but I don't think that's the same thing. It probably would not impact my body very directly.

8. Metaphysics, like we could have more than one thing like a blue blow pop but let's say they're not really the same thing, they could be completely different. If we have the collection of all such things, or a way of representing that we have included everything, then if we have the right system it could help us gain understanding. What does this have to do with blue blow pops anyway?

Question: <u>What theory was applied in the ultrasound blind walking stick project?</u>

I offered a Chinese longevity herb to my parents and they decided they didn't want it. It's untouched in their cabinet for probably 4+ years. My mother studied to be an RN and my stepfather is an aging computer programmer. You'd think they'd see benefits, right? But apparently immortality is just interesting to certain people, possibly mostly philosophers and Asian people. I personally would object to immortality if it involved taking a lot of injections.

...

"Even small amounts of lead could be very problematic. Some of the competing cultures weren't as mentally developed as the Greeks or Chinese. The Chinese are some of the smartest today." —<u>What conditions allowed for Greece to become the birthplace of Western philosophy, rhetorical devices (logos, ethos, and pathos), and modern science?</u>

People with good memories are hired relatively quickly.

Poor people who are highly creative thinkers may not like people.

Poor people who love people may not want to change their life.

Poor people tend to love people or hate people or test poorly on IQ.

The types of people hired for jobs are technical people, entertainers, people with good memories, and people with money.

—<u>Deconstructive IQ Test</u> (...)


"And, also, if it was material I was really interested in I actually found it easier to read that while listening to someone else, rather than reading something I didn't like while listening to someone." —<u>What makes it so difficult to read and listen to someone who is trying to have a conversation with you at the same time?</u>

<u>Theory of Complex Weight Gain, Schizophremia, and Dopamine</u> (...)

*November 14, 2020*

Maybe schizophrenics who prohibit themselves from eating sugar develop high dopamine. Maybe those who love sugar develop low dopamine to avoid diabetes. Maybe those who are not schizophrenic either avoid sugar or burn a lot of calories, or gain weight.

Note: Serotonin may be more important.

<u>Does higher intelligence correlate with brighter or more intense eyes?</u> (in my view, based on observation, no or not exactly, rather it indicates pain, vanity or drug use, or in some cases pleasure or sensitivity)

In my experience, shiny eyes are associated with drug use, and intense eyes are associated with staring in mirrors a lot.

I would view Tesla's eyes as deep but not intense.

My own eyes have varied from glossy and non-perceptive, to intense and wild, to glossy and soulless-looking, to somewhat more mature but a bit glossy.

The biggest connection I could find is that both pain and taking heavy drugs result in glossy eyes, whereas soulless eyes are created by not staring in the mirror at all, and intense eyes are created by staring in the mirror. Wild eyes are created by fight-or-flight. Glossy eyes also sometimes means sensitivity to drugs or pain.

All forms of wood products eventually cause complete blindness if consumed. This has been observed happening even with gorillas.

<u>Anything that avoids pain seems worth it</u>

*March 11, 2020.*

You get reborn as someone with more physical problems.

I think I was a crazy boy who thought his name was Euler around 1906. He probably had perfect memory but I don't remember now.

In some ways I was concealing my problems but in a way it was the perfect thing to do.

Not too many regrets at that point. But my next life was really evil, not famous evil it ended up getting involved in working in an underground camp, sometimes at gun-point. I thought I was oblivious, writing poetry. It was only about my 20th to 21st life, and I couldn't remember much. It was like I wasn't physical yet. I barely knew pain, then when I was shot I felt like my best option was to sell my soul to avoid it. I'm one and a half lives past that time now. It seemed serious then, it must still be serious, the idea of avoiding pain.

Now its like I have a Theory of Everything. But is it worth it? It just seems worth it to avoid the pain. Anything that avoids pain seems worth it.

<u>The first two people to answer about "If you had to risk everything, what would it be for" agree that long life and happiness are desirable goals</u>

*Feb 22, 2020.*

Only two things, immortality or perpetual motion machines.

Although I agree with Ssmuel Muldoon's answer somewhat, in some cases I would seek a long happy life without depression. It depends on circumstances.

My life has been painful but I have not been depressed, so I don't feel like I have to wish for happiness, it sounds too ironical somehow.

Immortality though is a wish for a long life the way most people look at it, and perpetual motion could make a lot of people happy.

<u>What is it like to have schizophrenia?</u>

*By June 19, 2019.*

I've been on one medication since 2003. Most schizophrenics are told they need more than one medication to 'manage the symptoms'.

I'm considered a serious case for having schizophrenia, but other than requiring medication, I'm mostly in remission, which in the case of schizophrenia doesn't mean that it's going away. It is a lifelong illness, even if I don't have any symptoms. That is literally what my psych prof told me (in real life).

I have a lot of beliefs that some would consider delusional, but some of them have a basis in reality. You might not believe that I time-traveled or invented perpetual motion, but you might have to believe that I published a book on Amazon called Socratic Writings, and that my philosophy, in particular Programmable Heuristics, might influence computer programmers. Otherwise, what? I'm probably not hallucinating the whole internet, or the websites called Twitter and Amazon.

It has been easier to cope with schizophrenia when I realized that I'm only smart enough or irrational enough to have full-blown hallucinations when I'm really stressed out. However, I tend to be always stressed out when I'm not on medication. Either stressed out or nearly catatonic. Engaging in abstract sketches and focusing on remembering dreams I had while I was asleep have been important activities for me even before I took medication.

It has been difficult to construct a life-narrative. I wanted to become a professor when I grew up (actually, it was not a very emotional commitment). When I went to college I learned my parents probably couldn't afford for me to attend for four years, and there was the 9/11 thing and I was in college in upstate New York, and it was a bit traumatizing. I didn't know what to believe, and it seemed like I needed to re-construct my own future before it had even happened.

I wanted to be an emotional, authentic person with a girlfriend, but I was skinny and effeminate and I couldn't even really prove I was a nerd. I was in a social ditch. It's not that schizophrenia was a choice, or not exactly, but in some ways it was the available route for me. If I didn't have schizophrenia, I would have better social skills, a sense of continuing fulfillment, and less need to re-construct my life.

Recently I have gone through some transformations which make me feel like maybe I can recover, even though doctors say that this illness is chronic and horrible. I have learned some basic things about calculus, and become more socially functional around people like my therapist and my mother.

I have negotiated to reduce my medication slightly, and unfortunately I have been hearing voices a little more than before, which is never a good sign, but I do feel I can fight them a little bit, but I'm not yet sure if I will improve enough to reduce any more.

My life focuses around my intellectual activities (I write almost every day on my blog with the aim of doing things like re-constructing the work of Socrates), attending school part-time (I recently reached Junior status after about 16 years), and trying to recover from schizophrenia by focusing on the things that most matter.

According to my therapist I'm doing extremely well for a schizophrenic. He says my perseverance is admirable. He even says over and over that I'm a genius, which is something I never expected him to say. All-in-all, I try to consider that there is no real way to absolutely objectify a diagnosis. As soon as someone understands themselves and takes life seriously, you have to treat them like a human being, and then it seems to me that even if being schizophrenic is very limiting, the whole person does not exist inside the diagnosis. And if that is the case, then there must be some way to be as sane, stupid, or spiritually enlightened as I was before the illness.

I will add that my mental experiences are not very wonderful. I feel a lot of grinding pain, but less than I felt when I was younger. This is a result of a childhood accident that I barely remember, combined with some abuse with a hammer that I received from my father and younger brother, and another time that I fell down a flight of stairs and saw my life in slow motion, and hit my mouth on a table at the bottom of the stairs, losing both front teeth.

However, I feel happy in the sense of not feeling emotionally depressed. I have never had depression. For that I am lucky. On the other hand, I have not been manic, or particularly socially-functional either. An honors student in high school, but not someone known for wit or popularity.

However, I do feel that I have a chance of being remembered for greatness in spite of my continual headache. It would even make my life make more sense. The 600K views on Quora, the fact that I am mentioned as famous quotable on <u>Poems - Quotes - Poetry</u> (Poemhunter, look under famous quotations number 61 currently). My many talents: philosophy, art, inventing, poetry, etc. My life has a lot of potential, and I wish sanity was part of it.

<u>Does history correctly assess those who get written into it?</u>

*Dec 30, 2019.*

This is a brilliant question, because

For one thing, there are a lot of respectable people in history.

For another thing, ordinary textbooks do little to analyze the baseness of humanity.

So, we are under an illusion they're all better people no matter what.

Meanwhile, what if someone with Turrett's Syndrome or a mental disability does something great?

History may hold an impossible standard to new people simply because the ancients weren't thought of as base and human.

So, the question is, do any of these new people do something great even with a disability?

I think the answer is yes. I'm one example.

I have a theory of everything. There is also evidence I have a broken head and a mental disorder.

Traditionally, a broken head would mean I don't have a theory of everything.

But are my words so wrong? What if it is the best theory after all?

That is the kind of question we have to consider.

In the age of chocolate and internet, are we going to measure up to the ancient ones?

Or, alternately, if humans aren't equal, why does it seem possible someone from a smart family with a broken head has the only Theory of Everything?

Or the only major evidence of perpetual motion so far, for that matter?

<u>Alternate Reality (Recommended)</u>

My experience of this is there are:

- Higher dimensions.
- Enlightened states.
- Different dimensions, for example the Mists of Time.
- Ways of seeing white light.
- Things similar to astral at least sometimes under some conditions.
- Un-located dream states.

The earlier ones may be harder to realize.

SUMMARY OF UNIVERSES WITH SUGGESTIONS ON HOW TO GET THERE:

1. The Plan of Nature is Purposeful Meaning

- Get involved with something basic, something full of purpose. Have plenty of time, and avoid nit-picking.

2. Quantified Qualia

- Analyze emotionally. Use visualization.

3. Clear Well Book of Shadows

- Know old beautiful people. Think of yourself outside of time. Consider phenomenological visions.

4. Desired Thought

- Think about your personality. Focus on the immediate boldness.

5. Metaphysical Animal

- Begin with poetry. Think of your own world. Connect the dots.

6. Abstract Industrialism

- Keep track of special vantages. Keep a brief survey of notations in your mind. Plan to return to the vantages.

7. Notes and Petals of Inspiration

- Think of the butterfly dream. View it superficially. Make something beautiful. Think everything is beautiful. Don't feel sad.

8. Karmaband

- View things seriously. Understand the irony. Explore the world. Have perspective, make judgments.

9. Radical Contingency

- Philosophy. Takeaway metaphor. Pure significance.

10. The Riddles of Truth

- The invisible is yet visible. Truth declares itself. Deeper things are something to appreciate. Water in one's hands.

11. Improvement through Advanced Ockham

- Connexions. Easy path of mind. What follows is the result. The result is divine.

12. Problematics

- What if there were a snarl, it might be interesting and symbolic.

13. Meaningful difference

- If you noticed something it might be important.

14. Fringe Ladders

- What you noticed might be an environment with symbolic locations.

15. Symbolic Exercise

- What you viewed before was purely formal, it could be both significant and insignificant.

16. Paradoxical Principles

- It gradually dawns, with dimensions there is a deeper level.

17. Great Suppositions

- Perhaps what was missing is what is great, what is fortunate, what is perfect, what is most highly interesting.

18. Perfect Immunity

- If you were to save yourself from significance, you would still want immunity. You would want a reserve card, something for definite.

19. Perfect Success

- The perfect thought is you could enter another condition, if you had the perfection which follows from immunity.

20. Complexity and Perfection

- After the second condition you might find another creativity. Finally you would be like God.

Integration of Raisins

From 'Writing on the Spirits' part II. Dated somewhere between 2016 - 2018.

Ostensibly God already answered the only question we wouldn't know the answer to when he created existence!

God was asking: 'What is nothing?' 'How can it be nothing?' 'What is divine about nothing?' Etc.

Asking questions about nothing with a lot of power is like creating reality.

Alternately, you might believe that reality is eternal and the nature of consciousness is the unsolved question.

However, it is possible to see that consciousness is a means to an end to some extent. Highly expensive, often slightly disappointing.

As soon as consciousness seems to become cheap, it bears fruit. At that point we can define consciousness as paradoxical.

To the primitive tool-building brain all that consciousness needs is a reason to live, and some form of technicalism to mull into thoughts, or some equivalent thing to turn into emotions, or both, etc.

At this point you may find it is easier to understand consciousness.

Consciousness is holy, so far as that is possible. It is also an attempt to process the worst problems, and to find the best solutions.

I think I have heard someone define it as 'a holy paradox'. Other definitions could be proposed, often relating to the soul, transformation, attributes, powers, and modes of existence.

## TRANSPERSONAL PSYCHOLOGY

Intro: Pan Optimism from Pan Psychology

- If it's one world as I proved by seeing my clone, then...
- If someone takes drugs, and someone else feels optimistic...
- Then it could explain why someone who didn't take drugs feels optimstic.
- But if the second person doesn't feel optimistic, It could mean something is wrong.
- And it could also be wrong to be addicted, for example someone else might steal your high.

0

Things like leadership, medical knowledge, good fighting skills, and wisdom seem too habitual to belong to just one life.

1

I understand that there are two different definitions.

I recognize that.

But the secret entities insist that I take damage, by their petty sense of justice.

By their sense of justice, I offer two definitions: one being their justice, and one being my own personal sense of self.

But that's back to two different definitions.

Then they blame me for having two definitions, and insist that I take damage.

And so on.

In an idealistic mentality, this sort of mental process would make dimensional urbanism look more idealistic, but in point of practice it causes interpersonal problems.

—Intellectual Schizophrenia

2

[Nathan's answer to: I have a brilliant memory. Do I have aphantasia?]

Poor liquid intelligence perhaps, or perhaps you're just over self-critical.

There are not a lot of people who can imagine anything they've seen. You might have a perfect visual memory or eidetic memory.

I'm personally not one to judge. My memory is very poor, and though I can visualize somewhat it's not too fantastic. Costs energy. And is usually creative rather than mnemonic.

I sort of have the opposite problem, I can't remember anything real, I can only create new things. Problem with this is that I'm open to manipulation, so if someone has way more visual memory they could probably enslave me to some obscure detail without me ever knowing.

—Nathan Coppedge's answer to I can imagine in my mind anything I have seen. However, I can't imagine anything I haven't seen previously. Do I have aphantasia?

3

It is interesting how if society helps INFPs, the world generally improves, sort of like a magic power. I'm referring to the INFP 'empathic' ability. (INFPs are often called 'Empaths').

Alternate Reality Experiences:

I think these actually happened:

- Yoda was omniscient, and I was asked to be inside his head. He said I was a little good but not good enough. It seemed to be interminable, and I wanted to escape. When I returned I was once again in my waking body.
- I spiritually visited the (Knights of the) Roundtable, and laughed with most of them at someone who looked like my future landlord. I felt like I was making an evil bargain.
- I visited a temple in an unknown place, and ordeted wine that didn"t taste like anything. This was in 2010, the year in which nothing happened (in 2009 everything happened).
- In high school I was sitting in the library with friends during lunch when I suddenly felt I was walking in the hallway above. I saw a sign that said Akashic Records (at the time I did not know what this meant at all), then an old man popped out of the door and said "I bet you don't

remember the apostrophe" then slammed the door. I then reappeared in the library.

- I was walking in Washington with my Dad and brother when it seemed that our Dad was telling us we would see a sculpture just like in the Keeno political cartoons. We arrived there rather quickly perhaps after a subway ride, and it indeed looked just like me and my brother both imagined it: a big giant made of stone sprawling over a circular walkway. Then we were about to leave when my heart felt a pull to make something more out of it, and lo and behold I felt a spiritual pull to understand Marie Antoinette, and in the sky we could see some type of bird-like things. What are they? My brother said. I think they're perpetual motion machines, I said. Impossible, my brother said. Where did they go, he said. Then my Dad said, you have to admit that was pretty cool. Then we were on an ordinary sidewalk in Washington.

- Twice I saw someone dressed as a ninja turtle climbing the stairway of a tall building as if they were trying to jump. This was real life, I was with my Dad and brother at least one of the times.

- Once I was in a sleeping bag. I was about 9 years old. Then I suddenly saw a terrifying vision of the Fates in concert. It seemed like a very big undergtound room with terrifying noise but very beautiful. When I woke up I realized I had almost suffocated.

ADAPTING:

- Female narcissists might give you reason to fear. This may be primarily why people say 'f*** you'.

## Sleep Studies

*July 26, 2020*

Reverie—Visionary sleep or suspension.

Solving the 'Sleep Demon': at night, something seems to feed on the back of the brain, causing drowsiness.

*Hypnagogia* experienced during the periods between wakefulness and sleep. It is characterized by flash visions and auditory stimuli that usually make no sense although the mind races really fast. ---Shalom Dickson

"With sleep and onset, expectations are neither more nor less than is normal." —thought to have been said by Hippocrates, founder of Greek medicine.

SLEEPY WORDS:

It's only a clear window.

The sword is too dangerous to have a real effect on me.

Sexually-injured Idealists

Here are some un-ideal sounding examples that may help figure this out. WARNING: Some graphic content, do not read ahead if you think sexual fetishes are offensive.

A woman dreams of marrying a professional weight-lifter. She does get married, but her husband is overweight. He can lift some things, but in some ways she ends up doing a lot of the work herself.

A man dreams of having sex with a woman with gigantic breasts. Instead his brother sees a prostitute who has average-size implants. Although he might have some attraction to the prostitute, all that is left of his passion is vicariousness, because he has erectile dysfunction from his medication.

These are examples of maximalism. In maximalism, one eventually comes to terms with the reality and settles for less. The reality might be totally different from imagination. For example, the man who had the fantasy might have just wanted vicarious pleasure. The woman who had the fantasy might just have wanted to get married to someone who carries the groceries occasionally. In maximalism, there is usually a lot of compromise.

Idealism on the other hand is not about reality at all. Idealism is more like the original fantasy. There could be a lot wrong with idealism that doesn't matter to the idealist. For example, a woman could like weight-lifters who remains single her whole life. A man could like gigantic breasts without even being called a real man.

Idealists compensate rather than compromising. The man for example, might collect a large number of comic books that originally help him fantasize, but eventually he just thinks they're a great collector's hobby. The woman might actually start lifting weights to compensate for not finding a strong man. These adaptations aren't really compromises, they're more like compensations. Sometimes, idealism never connects with anything remotely similar to the physical things that were desired.

On the other hand, in the abstract, the idealist might be satisfied. An idealist might become famous instead of having sex, or might become a man's boss instead of getting married.

With a true idealist though, the abstraction becomes detached entirely from the physical reality, to the point where they almost prefer pain over pleasure as long as they have abstractions. For example, a woman who has injured herself sexually may decide to work in a job that is located inside a tower, e.g. because it is hard for her to get an orgasm. Or, a man who has sexually injured himself may become devoted to big generalities instead of big breasts, e.g. because it is no longer possible the breasts are arousing enough and this process might begin developing during adolescence when they are only thinking about big breasts.

## An Argument that Medicine May Cause Delusions

*Dec 24, 2019.*

- In 2000 I had evidence of perpetual motion, not medicated. Although partly misunderstood by everyone including me at the time, the device I built showed evidence of natural torque perhaps from rest using exponential efficiency, not kidding you.
- In 2009 I took a break from meds and got my first inkling of the Characteristica Universalis, a quest uncompleted by Leibniz, who is said to have had a 200 IQ.
- By the time I made further progress on perpetual motion it was 13 years later than 2000, during which I took medication.
- By the time I made further major progress on universal knowledge from a scientific standpoint it was nine years later, during which time I was medicated.
- On the one hand, medication may have saved me from many dangerous and embarrassing encounters.

- On the other hand, my best un-medicated work seems to predate my best medicated work by an average of 11 years in all major categories.
- Now, say we have that information and we also learn I would still think I had been Marie Antoinette if I was un-medicated, but I am not sure of it. Keep in mind I did not think I was Marie Antoinette until nearly 20 years of medication.
- On top of that, let's say I found everything less believable when I was off my meds, as I observed, so the Marie Antoinette delusion would not be as serious.
- Now, if we claim the belief that I am Marie Antoinette is a delusion, then being off meds could be better, because I am more skeptical off meds, less willing to believe it's real.
- However, I'm also way better at producing meaningful work when I'm off meds according to the argument, which suggests I am clearer thinking without the meds.
- Now it looks like I'm clearer thinking, I'm less delusional, it looks then like the medicine is causing a delusion.

<u>Something Interesting about Fox and Hedgehog Philosophers</u>

*October 27, 2019.*

A basic survey indicated compatibility with William James but this was thought to be erroneous, because he went to Harvard.

A greater connection was found with psychologists such as Jung and Adler, but this was also thought erroneous because psychologists are known to run IQ tests.

Philosophers were shown to be attached to a wide variety of opinions, the more variety essentially the higher the intelligence. One conclusion was philosophers are attracted to describing as much information as possible rather than ascribing to a specific view.

Past this point, the conclusion was everyone who found philosophy relevant was a philosopher, so any time someone was smart and interested in philosophy, it meant they were some type of philosopher.

The study dead-ended in a simple analogy to foxes and hedgehogs. Like many academics, philosophers fell into two categories: fox and hedgehog (metaphors). The foxes tended to enjoy debate for its own sake, whereas the hedgehogs enjoyed the arguments. The difference with philosophers was that the further they went in one direction, the better they were able to take advantage of the OPPOSITE.

So, in philosophy, really extreme hedgehog generalists sometimes know a lot about the specifics of life. Yet, at the same time, really clever philosophers (foxes) tended to win at arguments (arguing being normally what hedgehogs are attracted to do).

Each was designed to beat the other in an exaggerated kind of way, almost like they both knew nothing about what the other was actually doing. Which is ironic, because philosophers are trying to understand everything.

However, it seemed to be the case that the very greatest philosophers almost always became hedgehogs or else foxes who had lost a lot of arguments. So, one conclusion was that the greatest hedgehogs rarely lost arguments, but the greatest fox philosophers won by trial and error.

So, great philosophers are good at being right, or else know how to take advantage of situations where they have lost the argument.

However, confusingly, the ones who won the argument were not the ones who were good at tricking people, and the ones who won by laborious trial and error were normally the ones who were trying to be tricky. So, it was like the boring stupid ones had become tricksters, and the tricksters had been led along in a painful process of re-educating themselves.

In conclusion, the greatest hedgehog philosophers were actually wise,

That's one conclusion.

But, perhaps I should have said, the greatest hedgehog philosophers were actually wise... or at least made others behave like they were.

So, either the hedgehogs were somewhat occult, or there was something foxes could learn from them, or philosophical foxes are not good at knowing what's right.

However, if we assume philosophical foxes are great arguers and take that as a sign that they are right, then it still seems the hedgehogs who are teaching them a lesson either have real knowledge or have occult power, maybe both.

However, one angle is that it may be that certain hedgehogs are way better than the average hedgehog, so it is not certain whether the knowledge hedgehogs have is held in common among many of them. So, it may just be that certain extremely rare hedgehog philosophers simply learn how to be *tricky hedgehogs*. To them, it just means being a philosopher, excluding the foxes.

So, as far as high IQ, if you're interested in philosophy, the choice is between extremely adapted people who are (diabolically?) correct about life, and people who learn what they need to learn in a finite number of steps.

<Sorry I don't have a source. I believe I heard it from my Dad, who is a Yale PhD and probably read it somewhere or heard it in a conversation with his students or colleagues.>

<u>Eccentric Beliefs, Schizophrenia, Occult Powers.
Childhood Accident</u>

*October 27, 2019.*

I don't know whether I reject verifiable knowledge or
not. I don't identify as a crackpot, but who would?

But, people might THINK that I reject empricism, but
really it's just that I'm not a scientist.

I do believe in some things occult.

For example, I can balance a fork on it's point on a
table long enough to photograph it:

Here is another one of some pants that I think I magically enchanted to stay upright against a bathroom counter:

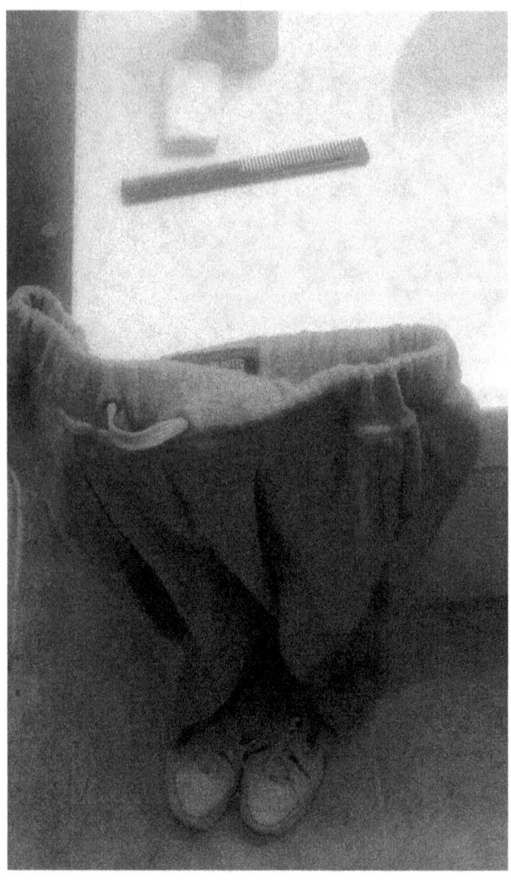

I have a lot of exceptional achievements which largely aren't publicly recognized, like a theory of everything and over 100 published books.

But if you want to know my diagnosis, I have been labeled with paranoid / undifferentiated schizophrenia which means I hallucinate (mostly what are called in common parlance imaginary voices), and have highly antisocial abnormal behavior (I wouldn't emphasize abnormal behavior, but other people would. In high school I would have called myself a conformist, the major difference now is I'm pursuing some talents and have a health problem) and I sometimes have uncontrollable crazy impulses if I don't take my meds. It means there's something wrong with my brain, in my case very little in the way of good sensations relative to my level of intelligence. Part of it is due to a childhood accident which probably couldn't be blamed on genes alone.

<u>What's an example of a psychopath who made a great discovery/invention?</u>

I was never diagnosed with psychopathy specifically, although my diagnosis of paranoid / undifferentiated schizophrenia implies episodes of madness, which in psychological parlance are called psychosis. For example, if someone stands on top of a radiator inside a hospital that is called psychosis because it is seen as irrational behavior.

My possible accomplishments might be notable given what I have found about scientific beliefs currently.

- The Theory of Everything.
- Method for predicting the past using important events.
- Formula for predicting important historical events.
- Characteristica Universalis.
- Unified Language Formula using mathematics.
- The Disintegral, a concept bridging psychology and physics.
- Objective Knowledge using coherence.
- General Solution to All Problems and Paradoxes.

- Formula for the soul of information on descriptions of two words or longer.
- Formula for Basic Meaning in information.
- Formula for Answering Questions Perfectly.
- Formula for Perfect Questions.
- Formula for predicting immortality.
- Theory of working perpetual motion machines.
- Contributions to Hyper-Cubist art movement.
- I have two poems that were rated 10 / 10 by more than one person.

Studying the Extremely Rare Case of an Intellectual
with Brain Damage

Something that might help you is that crystallized
intelligence is not pain. See if you can imagine that. I
have found that helps. I may have even gotten this
advice from a neoroscientist.

There are various things that can help if you have a lot
of pain in your head.

One of the biggest leaps that can be made is to study
crystallized intelligence and try to realize that your
head doesn't have to be broken.

I can give more advice if this explanation is making
sense.

To be more clear about why I am concerned, I myself
suffered a childhood accident when I was very young.
Even though I was an honors student, I struggled with
homework and ultimately developed a mental illness.

Some of the things that helped me on my way to
partially recover my brain were:

- Eating raw mango fruit, about age 3.
Everyday life: Dad is studying at Yale and doing
research at Princeton.

- I thought about broken pottery unconsciously, about age 9.
- I was introduced to the art of M.C. Escher, about age 11.

Everyday life: My parents are divorced, my brother is a prodigy in a gifted program.

- I discovered I could try to be intellectual, age 18.

Everyday life: I go to a private college and get good grades but develop a mental illness.

- My Dad told me about the accident, and I decided to try to repair my head using a mixture of biology and telekinesis, age 24.
- I discovered I could choose to eat fish, age 25.

Everyday life: I had a part-time job at the public library where I am initially paid far above minimum wage, but lose my job after two years.

- I started drinking a lot of tea, age 26.

Everyday life: I am spending time in cafes all the time, using my laptop, and supported by the U.S. Social Security program. It seems like a new age of freedom.

- I discovered a stuffed animal to be my personal familiar, age 26.

- I admired certain round thistles that fell from trees because they made me feel safe, this was an epiphany at age 26. And I dared to remember my brain damage.

Everyday life: My mother wants me to study to be a nursing assistant who cleans people's behinds. While I think this is an irrational idea, I go ahead and earn a CNA license, but no employment results as I am terrified of venereal diseases and think it's bad karma to be around old people. But then I get an amazing offer to move to a subsidized new modern apartment, and I set my hopes on being a successful author.

- Age 31, I finally took what I thought was a real algebra class in college, and got a B+ or above. The class was meaningful because it was taught by the same person who taught my smart friends calculus in high school, so I felt a kind of humble hopefulness that it might be possible to learn advanced math. I didn't know this, but algebra is an important step in developing intelligence, but I just felt that I had turned over a new leaf.

Everyday life: This was the year I discovered objective knowledge and my first major evidence of perpetual motion machines.

- Age 32, I tried drugs which were supposed to help with immortality. These actually ended up increasing my productivity and helping my school memory. But since I was pursuing a philosophy degree math was not really on the horizon. So, I began a big semantics project.

Everyday life: 2015 was my first productive year.

- Age 33, seeking metaphors for a more functional brain, I recovered my memory of a calculus lesson I had heard many years before from the high school hallway. This was a big step because my Dad loves calculus so it seemed like an ultimate goal of repairing my brain.
- Age 33, I also found a coin which appeared to turn to gold in my hands, which turned my interests more towards alchemy than math.
- Age 34, In a psychology class I discovered Crystalline Intelligence which was a big step but a bit subtle for me at first and still requires good luck and concentration even now. The important thing was not only that it helped intelligence,

> but that something that could break
> didn't have to hurt.
> - Age 36 I thought of myself as
>   founding a movement almost every
>   day, and found some fulfillment
>   describing the beginnings of the
>   authentic art of enchantment.
>   Sometimes I seemed to be able to
>   change the color of the sky by will,
>   usually to lavender.

Everyday life: I discovered The Theory of Everything.

The point is, in my case after my accident barring some kind of genuine panacea without these incremental steps beginning with eating mangoes there would be no way to reach this level of achievement unless I got even more authentic help with my brain. And it is strange to realize in a magical kind of way, if I didn't have a damaged brain I might have achieved much more.

It's easy to forget that a lot of our experience is internal and self-reinforcing.

If you experienced brain trauma at an early age like I did, you would still be in touch with some of your 'baby hormones' for developing your skull structure. That stuff is indeed real, and I imagine to some degree every part of our reality comes out of outer experiences and our own internal makeup.

Possibly quantum exploration of genus-species
relations increase brain activity in relation
to: <u>Impossible Quantum Problems</u>

1

We don't have common understanding, that might be
why there's a lot of pain. It's not because we need
common understanding, it's because we need less.
But maybe we don't survive with less. Maybe
quantumly we would know the negative space if we
knew less. Maybe entropy says what actually
happened is necessary.

Human reports on aliens: <u>Nathan Coppedge's answer to What if there is other kind of life but in different dimension?</u>

Here is what I know on this:

- If my past life as Kwang Kuo was correct, I was once examined in a higher dimension and could see nothing.
- Many Americans have reported contact with unusual species and being examined in the dark, which sounds similar.

A later guess I made 11,000 years after Guo suggests women, witches, and other compromising-yet-privileged people have advantage in the species.

Another guess suggests a set of three or more 'distant presences' who wish for humans to not sleep, not cry and comprehend.

Other than that, the latest prescription seems to be:

God suffers.

Why not change?

Why not change, and not become God?

It is ethical to change.

It is ethical to have a different God.

The morals of God.

—<u>The Ethics of Change</u>

<u>Conjecture How many new discoveries about the world are made each year?</u>

Major discoveries seem to have gone up from 3 to 5 per year over the last 30 years.

Although, science seems to have gone on overdrive with quantum computers and now seems to have 3 - 5 major stories every day now which would mean about 1000+ great discoveries a year.

General knowledge, a broader category, might have more than 20 discoveries per year although most of these are minor.

Personal discoveries might have as many as 100 million or more per year in the US alone.

## What is the relation of I.Q. and Culture?

Scientists have found out that good behavior is 50% I.Q. and 50% culture.

So, theoretically, a genius with no breeding could behave just as well as a highly cultured person with an average I.Q.


## Value of Vegetarianism

Are you a vegetarian?

This question virtually by itself measures intelligence, virtue, level of maturity, level of health, level of knowledge of languages, and the list goes on. There is a sense where everything good is vegetarian.

Age 16:

Vegetarian? No.

Interests: Sketchy Military Weapons.

Age 36

Vegetarian? Mostly.

Interests: Art, Languages, Philosophy, Perpetual Motion Machines.

<u>Case Example: Subjectivity of Respectfulness in the United States</u>

The difficult answer is...

Intersubjectivity involves the common condition of society, it's norms and values, the perception of one person by another, internal events translating one's function in society and one's role with other people. For Kant, it is an element which is vitally rational, in effect joining the unknown with the internal experience. It is the rational-that-is-perceived, so to speak.

Respect is a term which may appear subjective to some. The usual things come into play:

- Assumptions based on culture and status.
- Gender identity related things.
- Mental peculiarities of individuals.
- Abilities to interpret, reflect, and be creative.

I'm not saying it is completely subjective, but it is true that some people think 'respect' is an important, almost dominant concept, whereas others would consider it merely a diminutive part of social graces. Some people are asocial or come off as rude, and they would not find respect to be a very important concept. I'm not saying they wield social clout by being asocial or rude, I'm just saying that there are some people, even people who might seem polite, for whom the world picture is composed of many very different things than respectfulness.

For some, for example, respectfulness is a formal property like dressing up or learning etiquette. For others it is about appreciating one's own family. For others it is about enjoying the company of friends. Depending on what perspective is adopted or granted by life, one's assumptions and opinions about respectfulness may vary widely.

African Americans I find sometimes have a warped perspective on respectfulness because they love the idea of using the word 'respect' like 'give respect' in place of terms like 'respectfulness' or 'veneration'. To a white person, 'give respect' might look like a gangster rap mentality of like 'tough you're dead', which doesn't look anything like etiquette or what white people would call respectfulness.

For what is traditionally called white culture, respectfulness looks very serious and impersonal like being quiet in church. Most whites would probably say that respectulness is identical to politeness, at a stretch real humility. For traditionally black culture, respectfulness looks more like egotism and self-betterment, a status symbol. Most African Americans would probably say respectfulness is like honor or privilege. These two perspectives seem to show that respect is partly a subjective concept.

For amusement, see also the non-racially biased writing: <u>What issues will divide the world into two even opposing camps?</u>

<u>Did research find that high school students perform better on tests if they are in a classroom with a view of a green landscape?</u>

No, I think embarrassingly researchers found students performed just as well, or perhaps even worse.

But their mental health improved.

Universal Basic Income Case Study

I know from experience.

Almost 100% of my income currently comes from SSI state unemployment benefits and SSA serious mental health disability.

1. I can pay cheap rent, so I don't currently have to live with my mother.
2. I have leisure time to.work on some of the best things that ever happened (perpetual motion, valuable philosophy, abstract art).
3. I can afford food.
4. I'm not so desperate that I do anything criminal or stupid.
5. I have a sense of humanity.

It costs the government less than it would cost to put me in prison from crimes I didn't currently commit, and I think they collect a lot of money on the local rent subsidy program, maybe about net $24,000 on my $690, more than I collect on Social Security.

I think I heard once 23,(000) is the golden number.

<u>Approaching Adult Problems with Childlike Creativity due to Accident</u>

*By what mechanism are perpetual motion machines supposed to function and have we even come close?*

*July 9, 2019.*

Not everyone seems to know how they work. I just seem to have the brain for it.

Both my grandfathers were engineers, and then I got a childhood accident, preserving some of my 'early creative thinking' brain. Although some of my functions were inhibited, designing perpetual motion machines was not one of them.

However, I started thinking of designs late, mostly after the age of 24. This allowed me to recover some of my mental function, approaching adult problems with a child-like intelligence. In fact, I still have a stuffed animal who is my dearest friend and for me he is like my child.

<u>Meaningful Case Studies</u>

1

There are people whose ears don't protrude.

What do they do, puff away?

I have a right to ask the question of what happens to other people?

2

I don't want to be a zombie, a soldier, a victim, or an animal, nor do I want to be in any dicey situations, nor do I want to be hideous, nor do I any longer want to suffer in the lower classes.

3

What is the rage these days? What if it were the rage, the rage you know?

What happens when people take standards seriously?

What will happen if life becomes reliable?

Good, you know?

4

What plagues you?

Anything, anything at the end of the day?

What mysteries do we imagine which almost hurt us, but occur to us when we are almost relieved of this plague?

How can we cure ourselves of this mystery?

Someone said once I was strung out on mystery as usual, but I did not know the truth. You see, they want me to perform absurd tricks, not the tricks they think of.

They make me perform absurd tricks, but it is not the tricks they think of.

The mysterious is the difference, but it is not the truth of either side of the difference.

So, I wish to cure a plague. I don't know if mystery must be cured. Maybe or not. It is not the whole truth. This has always been obvious to me.

<u>Diary of my mental chemistry</u>

May 12, 2019

My personal experience is there were some good things about 1982 - 1990 but it was mostly pure hell that I couldn't come to terms with, yet bland and boring on the outside, then things kind of held constant experientially from 1991 - 1995. Around 1996 I began to feel a little different about life, and things improved slightly until 2001 when I went to college. In college life seemed suddenly bad, fully of zombie-people who would not help me. By 2003 I was on medication and hearing voices in my head. However, I began drinking more tea and eventually Starbux chai tea and by 2010 my chemical mood had improved immensely with greater ability for nuanced feeling. Beginning in 2011 I was able to work on large books and other projects. In 2013 I had some big achievements, and in 2014 - 2015 I published many books per year and began taking a Chinese herb to help with longevity. My mood was stable enough through all these years to never need medication for depression or bipolar disorder, and this trend continued, which I owe to not drinking coffee. 2016 - 2019 were some of my most prolific years ever mostly on my Quora blog, particularly 2018. My YouTube channel began to get about 20 views / day for the first time in 2019. I also crossed 1000 followers on

Quora, passed 2 million views on Quora, and my Amazon author check started paying out more than $20 / month which made a difference for me. Also, the Social Security Administration and Department of Social Services stopped bothering me so much about filling out paperwork this year, which made a huge difference in my quality of life.

For reasons like this, the years 2010 - 2019 have been a much better experience than any prior decade of my life. However, the point in time when the shift really began to occur was rooted in 2006 when I made a conscientious effort to biologically or telekinetically reverse the damage my skull had received during a childhood accident. For the first time, by 2009 or so, I wasn't feeling a constant extremely sharp pain in my head, and this became the basis for some of the mild mental experiences which resulted in much improvement. By contrast for most of the 1980's and 1990's or up until 2006 my life was purely awful.

If we assume people receive similar treatments, then we could generalize some of this across populations. But I think there are some people who enjoyed earlier times and think of them as the height of their life. But possibly some of these things like feeling painful feelings during the Clinton administration or entering a mini-dark age during 2001 - 2002 are pretty common. However, I think some of the people who drank coffee in the 1990's are probably having some pretty bad moods during this same time that I am feeling highly prolific.

Approaching Adult Problems with Childlike Creativity due to Accident

October 27, 2019

I try to imagine how life would be for someone else, and it must be we are ships passing in the night. But that is a scary idea, but I admit it is highly likely.

I have important ideas, but that doesn't mean necessarily that I have perfect perspective, at least not inherently.

Sometimes this type of egotism can be a bad sign within 20 years. I try to realize, but I'm not 40 yet... 1 to 3 years to go, and I will probably have to earn more money to make me stupid... Or I will start going crazy...

## A casual case-study on schizophrenia and depersonalization

I was much like that in the early 2000's, my exact belief system.

I discovered people's noses looked like their ears, and their ears like their noses, and I was almost hit by moving automobiles that weren't there.

I was already diagnosed with a mental health problem, but I still thought that some of my impressions were psychic powers that gave me hidden knowledge of reality.

The good news is, even though I eventually had to take psych meds, I found a relatively good choice for my psych med, Risperdal, because I told the clinician that I came from a smart family, my Dad is a Yale PhD, which is true. I also have been able to reject the anti-depressants they have offered me a few times, so I am not officially depressed yet at the age of 35—which means I'm doing pretty good from the standpoint of the depressed people (unless they hate schizophrenia).

In 2006 - 2009 I was hospitalized a few times for my mental condition. Throughout the process I was working on abstract art and little self-printed booklets of intellectual writings. Although I'm still in college I have become kind of famous on Quora (1.8 million+ views and 966+ followers, by no means guaranteed for most people), and my philosophical knowledge has recently expanded immensely with such works as an extensive online History of Philosophy, and works on systems theory, coherent systems theory, and many other topics.

Life is worth it and I wish I had developed some of these talents a few years sooner maybe with better ability to make my mind enjoy itself.

I'm posting this as a link on one of my pages, so for the records,

My personality is INfP: Introverted, Intuitive, Mildly Feeling, Perceptive.

Age: 35 years old.

Race: 1/2 English, 1/4 Irish, 1/4 German.

Health Problems: Paranoid Schizophrenia, Mild Allergies, Unused Prescription Eye-Glasses, Hives (Very mild genetic skin condition involving bumps like mosquito bites that appear when skin is irritated), Damage to Temporal-Frontal Region from Childhood Accident.

Pre-Linguistic Thinking

I suppose, in my best approximation...

Pre-lingual ideas are exaggerated, non-reduced, un-pejorative, fresh, not internally manipulated, glanced, overshadowing, pre-cognitive or pre-interpretational, youthful or maladaptive, wiped away with any further thought.

These thoughts often involve such things as unquestioned bigness, bravery of danger, tranquility of innocence for natural dangers, faithful symbiosis with nature, idolization of an enemy, and assumptions of commonly-shared ideas of people typically people-who-abide-here huh-thats-how-it-is kinds of thoughts.

Note also that this tends to be only the high level of functioning for pre-language. Much more of the time there might be overwhelming fear, physical damage, regret, a desire to escape or die, spiritual madness, strange difficult undeniable notions, an idea of how not to think, etc.

<u>What ways have been identified through research to be effective to teach scientific communication skills in English, and writing skills?</u>

I think the research said in the case of science, some people just don't have the ability at all and it can't be taught to those people. But there are some middle cases, but they rarely advance science proper.

In the case of English some skills can be taught through exposure like in other languages, but as usual for most complex languages, some people never reach high performance.

## Visual Shapes As Basis for Studying Human Advancement

1. Hallucination.
2. Mirage.
3. "Visions".
4. Holograms.
5. Illusions of depth / distance.
6. Warped mirrors.
7. Op-Art (similar to 4-d art).
8. Movies / Fantasy art.
9. Depth / distance.
10. Perspective drawing.
11. Eroticism / psychology.
12. Abstraction.
13. Symbolism.
14. Concentricity (shapes within shapes).
15. Zig-zags.
16. Curved lines.
17. Crossing lines.
18. Parallel lines.
19. Dots.
20. Triangles.
21. Circles.
22. Squares.
23. Randomness.

## The Problems with New Haven: A Personal Case-Study

I will just bring up the point that New Haven, CT may have a high I.Q. average and some of the best public and private schools, and a relatively good art scene (not as good as New York or San Francisco, but some of the cafes exhibit artwork for free, and people occasionally make sales if they're good), but New Haven is a famously bad place to live compared to many college towns. Its just not much fun, there's not much going on, a lot of the 'cool' people decide to move away to almost anywhere.

My guess is that there's something about New Haven that gives people headaches. I had to become this kind of notorious stupid genius on the internet before I regained some of my mental functions in New Haven. Some people are generally weird, or take drugs... New Haven is kind of generally *stupid*.

So, based on New Haven, it is impossible to judge intelligence by so-called cerebral integrity. A small amount of improved emotions would make a big difference for New Haven, but that doesn't mean people aren't smart. Many of them look intelligent as long as they are in New Haven, but would not function in Vermont or Montreal.

So, I would place more emphasis on emotions than many are willing to. Intuition is great. Being nice to people is great (this is more like Vermont or Montreal, hypothetically. New Haven is superficial). But people with those qualities of intuition and being nice sometimes have problems, too.

Its sort of like New Haven is designed for aspiring writers—people who don't need to interact with people. All it is is a process to develop good writing. But some of them are really bad at it. So there is a sense, after 30+ years in New Haven, of feeling it is just an empty husk designed for aspiring writers. And that makes it look totally superficial. I can see why some people in New Haven are depressed—they are not good writers.

<u>Philosophical consciousness</u>

This question is a little inappropriate, because like all humans, there is likely to be a broad range of awareness, and it is hard to say what is most valuable or perceptive.

I suppose there might be a number of categories that are best suited to tackling this question, i.e. types of perceptive philosophers:

- Philosophers good at original logic, like Saul Kripke or David K. Lewis, or maybe me.
- Philosophers good at math, like Leibniz or Rene Descartes.
- Philosophers such as ethicists and social theorists who are great at understanding other human beings, such as F.A. Hayek and public intellectuals.
- Philosophical people who score high in intuition and prediction, like aphorists, economists, and scientists.
- Philosophers who have become relative masters of their own systems and to a lesser extent, philosophers who successfully study the ancients or continue the work of

contemporaries, like Hegel, Husserl, and Neoclassical philosophers.
- Philosophers with knowledge of contemporary issues, sort of like Ray Kurzweil or Luciano Floridi are philosophers of contemporary issues.

<u>Case Studies: Overeating</u>

*July 17, 2019*

When no one noticed I was a horse, I didn't notice I still ate like a horse.

When I didn't think I was a dog, I wasn't a dog.

When I didn't think I ate like a pig, I was still fat.

A Sense of the Phenomenal Relation of Eidetic Visions
and Schizophrenia

She might have a much longer sense of ritual than I
have.

Geese like fleece with frozen bees.

Bees at peace.

Piece of bees, swimming with the geese.

And if she thinks that's crazy, she might act out.

Not to mention there are five and a half memory
temples, and the world is getting weirdly like
spaghetti.

Because its raining and we talked about Angeletti.

That's pretty fast treatment—I mean, God! Don't have
a coma


Anita Sanz: has a really small brain, but can do things
others can't do, according to my Dad, a Yale PhD

<u>Do some people innately smile, or is an acquired skill?</u>

I think it's partly brain development, and parrly whether emotions are viewed as internal or external.

A more embarrassed, introverted, or sometimes brain-damaged person is more likely to view emotions as exclusively internal, 'recovery events'.

<u>Could anyone act or live without belief?</u>

Yes, they can have a pain in their head that they have no assumptions about.

I know from experience. Its called cheap unattachment.

However, it is not the same thing as saying nothing is true, it simply means you are neither skeptical nor have any specific belief about what is or isn't going on.

<u>Philosophy of Personality</u>

If their parents drink coffee, they may give up on achieving outward happiness.

If their parents identify as wealthy, they will probably think life is about an impossible character development.

If their parents are artistic, they may think originality is an unattainable dream.

If their parents have an average job, they may become criminals.

If their parent kills themselves, they will try to burn themselves out and may also commit suicide.

In none of these cases will persuasion to the contrary prove fully effective.

—How do you foster a sense of creativity in children that will stay with them their whole lives?

<u>The Dark Side</u> (...)

In other words, The Dark Side. "What if it were called Dark World instead? Maybe everyone would feel better." —A devilish genius

SOVIET HAPPINESS EXPERIMENT

Story of the very evil or some would say very ironically 'good' experiment: Chloe Zhao's answer to What are some of the creepiest experiments ever done in human history?

It's possible these monstrous creatures resulting from the experiment were called 'the sleepers'.

Charlatanism, interesting. That's seems to convey some of what you meant.

Psychologists knew it was good. They said, they really loved that stuff. Humans are just animals or they would respond better.

Some argue though that something went very wrong with the experiment. That they weren't really human beings. They were REPLACED. By aliens, or more like demons.

It could be a sign of something very bad going on in society, something probably worse than psychopathy by the ordinary definition of psychopathy if there is one.

One of the more bizarre theories is the test subjects were parasitized by special maggots who could change someone's whole gene structure to maintain a flow of powerful chemicals into the maggots' bodies.

Real life is priceless? That's what I learn with schizophrenia, too.

Someone said, maybe it's a lie, concealing a really big horrible experiment.

https://apnews.com/article/health-oddities-ap-top-news-lung-cancer-cancer- [clues about how to treat grey hair]

Feral child intelligence test

*March 14, 2019.*

Maybe?

- Reaction-time (good) versus excessive food dependence (bad).
- Level of confusion (bad) versus complex behavior (good).
- Ability to avoid or limit intake of food that makes them look moody, castaway, or irritated if they eat it.
- Ability to engage in search behavior and notice and investigate unusual features of a room.

Of course, there may be no way of knowing whether they are starving or if they have been through trauma unless you consult a doctor or psychologist, otherwise the results could be wrong.

A very hungry child is doing a smart thing to eat greedily in some situations, and it is not about whether they say if they are starving or not.

Someone traumatized is going to be less likely to explore because in their experience the environment is threatening, and they may have reason to think it's foolish to explore.

Laser and fan multiverse experiement: <u>New, Similar Experiments Dramatically Achieve Rainer Plaga Suggestion To Prove Parallel Universes</u>

<u>Notes on Nathan's Idiosyncratic Intelligence</u>

What has universality must have reality: exceptions are the rule.

A complex approach that has understanding will be opposed by simple misunderstandings.

'Of course not' it turns out, is not a good beginning for any good idea!

Strange identities have potent properties.

<u>What experimental sources of error are unavoidable in psychological research?</u>

As far as clients, mixture of:

- Offending clients.
- Mis-classifying.
- Over-simplifying.
- Stupefying.

<u>Why isn't intelligence a measurable, quantifiable thing?</u>

Well, it could be, I guess.

But there are some factors:

- Time management. Some high-IQ people are too distressed or selfish to do the right thing. Also, there may be better uses of their time.
- Pleasure: Geniuses don't always have more fun, for example they may be depressed or have migraines. On the other hand, they may also want enjoyment more than anyone else because they're smart.
- Black swans: some ideas and inventions might not be predictable without direct experience with obscure subjects. Also, a genius might like obscure fields more than obvious discoveries.
- What's in it for me: not all big discoveries pay well, so the genius might not be credited for it.

Ether. It's kind of real. I saw some emerge from my groin. —<u>What is the strangest scientific theory that you know of?</u>

...

(People who save the world look pretty / handsome?)

[Credit: wikipedia]

I realize the only other man who has looked so pretty is Stanislav Petrov, the man who saved the world. This may not be a coincidence. Perhaps there is good in store for me after all!!! Could we call this the 'science' and 'liberal arts' versions of handsome?

—<u>The trail to fame by Nathan Coppedge</u>

—<u>Modern-Day Pangloss</u>


PERPETUAL MOTION ON YOUTUBE

"The more people hear an idea or see an event, the easier it is to believe or at least question its validity rather than reject outright." —Leta Rosetree

"The interesting thing is, in this case that is not completely true. Instead of seeking to verify evidence, youtube users have sought to verify what they already believe. They have stayed mostly in two separate camps: people who *choose* to believe, and people who *choose* to disbelieve. It is sort of how religion used to be." —Nathan Coppedge

## AN EXPLANATION OF MURDEROUS IMPULSES

Is if someone hurts their head as a baby, they may get frozen thinking little boys are adults (e.g. because the baby's brain doesn't develop quickly). If little boys are like adults to them, and little boys would need to terrify someone to act like adults in an adult world, then the person with brain damage assumes they need to do scary things to be an adult. But only if they have brain trauma. Similarly, if the connection is drawn to simply needing to recover 'baby resources' because of the traumatic accident, psychotic behavior might develop also with people who are abused, and with people who experience oxygen deprivation from drugs or taking plane flights as a baby.

## UPSTANDING HYPOTHESES (HYPOTHESES ON THE PROGRESSIVE MODEL)

Dystopianism—I think humans are basically at Medieval level, except feeling dumb from all the drugs. Cyborgs will probably go extinct, because it has all the characteristics of rejecting human genetic material.

If Isis had big breasts but was 2-dimensional, and women have 3-dimensional breasts now, then there is no reason to believe in the consistency of reality.

DOWNSTANDING HYPOTHESES (HYPOTHESES ON THE REJECTION MODEL)

If basic inventions are seen as too antiquated, too 'old and scary'. This could be summed up as mortality as a function of evolution. Some symbols represented by technology may be too scary to be compatible with instinct.

SOME EXPERIMENTS THAT MAY HAVE BEEN RUN ON NATHAN LARKIN COPPEDGE:

- Sometimes Nathan wonders if his left hemisphere was removed or didn't develop, because the right half of his brain appears to be heavier than the left half of his brain. Nathan may have also taken a lot of damage to his cognitive pleasure sectors and memory sectors. He also doesn't have very good math skills.

Weirder:

<u>Limbo</u>

*Does the fact that something exists imply the existence of a being who enables something to exist?*

No, not usually.

The concept of entity applies equally to dirt atoms and to humans. Although something could come from a person, or emerge from dirt, that is the exception to the rule, as not all things are humans and things don't usually emerge from dirt all the time.

Then science adds additional qualifications, and we are left to wonder whether there is another way. Maybe at another time, or if you're the right person, but not usually right now, or not obviously.

Does Limbo exist is the kind of question. Have you actually been there, or was it a disney cartoon? I suppose I don't know. Maybe, or maybe only recently. But the cartoon was recent, too.

ADDITIONAL LINKS:

- <u>History of Psychology</u> (Coppedge)
- <u>Sheaffer Williams's answer to Is it true that natural redheads need more anesthetic than normal? If it is true, what is the reason?</u>
- <u>Gareth Morgan's answer to Why do we humans have a nose that protrudes from our face and is easily broken? If we evolved from apes, then our noses should have a similar structure, right?</u>
- <u>Terry Lambert's answer to What makes a chimera? in Science - Next Generation</u> (...)

,,,

RECOMMENDED READING

Scientific Papers

Scientific Theories

The Dimensional Immortality Toolkit

The Dimensional Biologist's Toolkit

The Critical Body

The Best Advice on Various Subjects

Collected Quotations of Nathan Coppedge

## BIO

Nathan Coppedge or Nathan Larkin Coppedge (b.1982) , is a philosopher, artist, inventor, poet, and member of the international honor society for philosophers. A prolific author with over 200 books published on Amazon, he is a perpetual motioneer, famous quotable, and internationally-selling Hyper-Cubist. A one-time member of Tesla Society UK online and PESWiki, and founder of many Facebook groups, he lives near Yale University.